Happy Mothers
Day

To

Mom

From

Marcia

Date

5/16/17

for MOM *with* LOVE

Words to Warm a Mother's Heart

Pi Pocket
INSPIRATIONS

Ellie Claire
gift & paper expressions

...inspired by life
EllieClaire.com

Ellie Claire® Gift & Paper Expressions
Brentwood, TN 37027
EllieClaire.com
Ellie Claire is a registered trademark of Worthy Media, Inc.

For Mom, with Love
© 2015 by Ellie Claire
Published by Ellie Claire, an imprint of Worthy Publishing Group, a division of Worthy Media, Inc.

ISBN: 978-1-63326-017-7

All rights reserved. No part of this book may be reproduced in any form, except for brief quotations in printed reviews, without permission in writing from the publisher.

Scripture taken from: The Holy Bible, New International Version®, niv® Copyright © 1973, 1978, 1984, 2011 by Biblica, Inc.® All rights reserved worldwide. The Holy Bible, New King James Version® (nkjv). Copyright © 1982 by Thomas Nelson, Inc. The New American Standard Bible® (nasb), Copyright © 1960, 1962, 1963, 1968, 1971, 1972, 1973, 1975, 1977, 1995 by The Lockman Foundation. The Holy Bible, New Living Translation (nlt) copyright © 1996, 2004, 2007 by Tyndale House Foundation. Used by permission of Tyndale House Publishers Inc., Carol Stream, Illinois 60188. *The Message* (msg). Copyright © 1993, 1994, 1995, 1996, 2000, 2001, 2002. Used by permission of NavPress Publishing Group. Amplified Bible (amp) Copyright © 1954, 1958, 1962, 1964, 1965, 1987 by The Lockman Foundation. All rights reserved.

Excluding Scripture verses and deity pronouns, in some quotations references to men and masculine pronouns have been replaced with gender-neutral or feminine references. Additionally, in some quotations we have carefully updated verb forms and wording that may distract modern readers.

Stock or custom editions of Ellie Claire titles may be purchased in bulk for educational, business, ministry, fundraising, or sales promotional use. For information, please e-mail info@EllieClaire.com

Compiled by Jill Olson
Cover and interior design by Jeff and Lisa Franke | www.art-lab-studios.com

Printed in China

1 2 3 4 5 6 7 8 9 – 19 18 17 16 15 14

Table of Contents

Gratitude 2

God Bless You...6

The Beauty of Life 12

The Gift of Simplicity 18

My Heart Is Content 24

The Richness of Friendship...............................30

Providing All Our Needs 36

Wisdom to Live By..42

Covering of Prayer 48

A Mother's Influence 54

Taking Time to Love 60

God Our Father 66

Thank You, Lord!...72

Living in Truth 78

Spirit of Joy 84

To Live, Laugh, and Love 90

The Strength of Family 94

I Believe...100

Be Encouraged 106

Special Gifts We Share.....................................112

Love Eternal 118

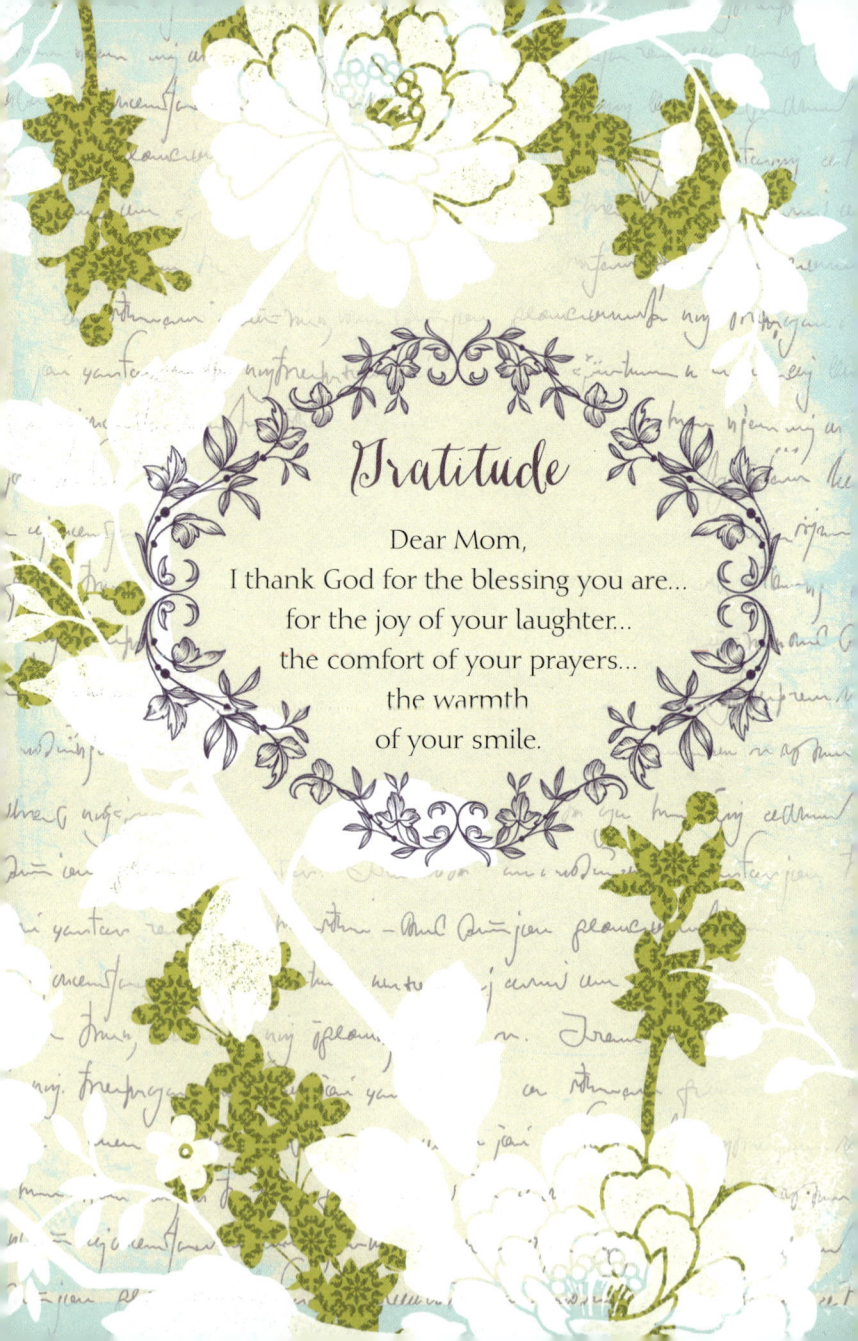

Gratitude

Dear Mom,
I thank God for the blessing you are...
for the joy of your laughter...
the comfort of your prayers...
the warmth
of your smile.

A mother is the truest friend we have,
when trials heavy and sudden fall upon us;
when adversity takes the place of prosperity;
when friends desert us; when trouble thickens
around us, still will she cling to us, and endeavor
by her kind precepts and counsels to dissipate
the clouds of darkness, and cause peace
to return to our hearts.

Washington Irving

All I am I owe to my mother.

George Washington

I will praise you, Lord,
with all my heart…
I will sing your praise.
I will bow down
toward your holy temple
and will praise your name
for your unfailing love
and your faithfulness

Psalm 138:1–2 niv

I remember my mother's prayers
and they have always followed me.
They have clung to me all my life.

Abraham Lincoln

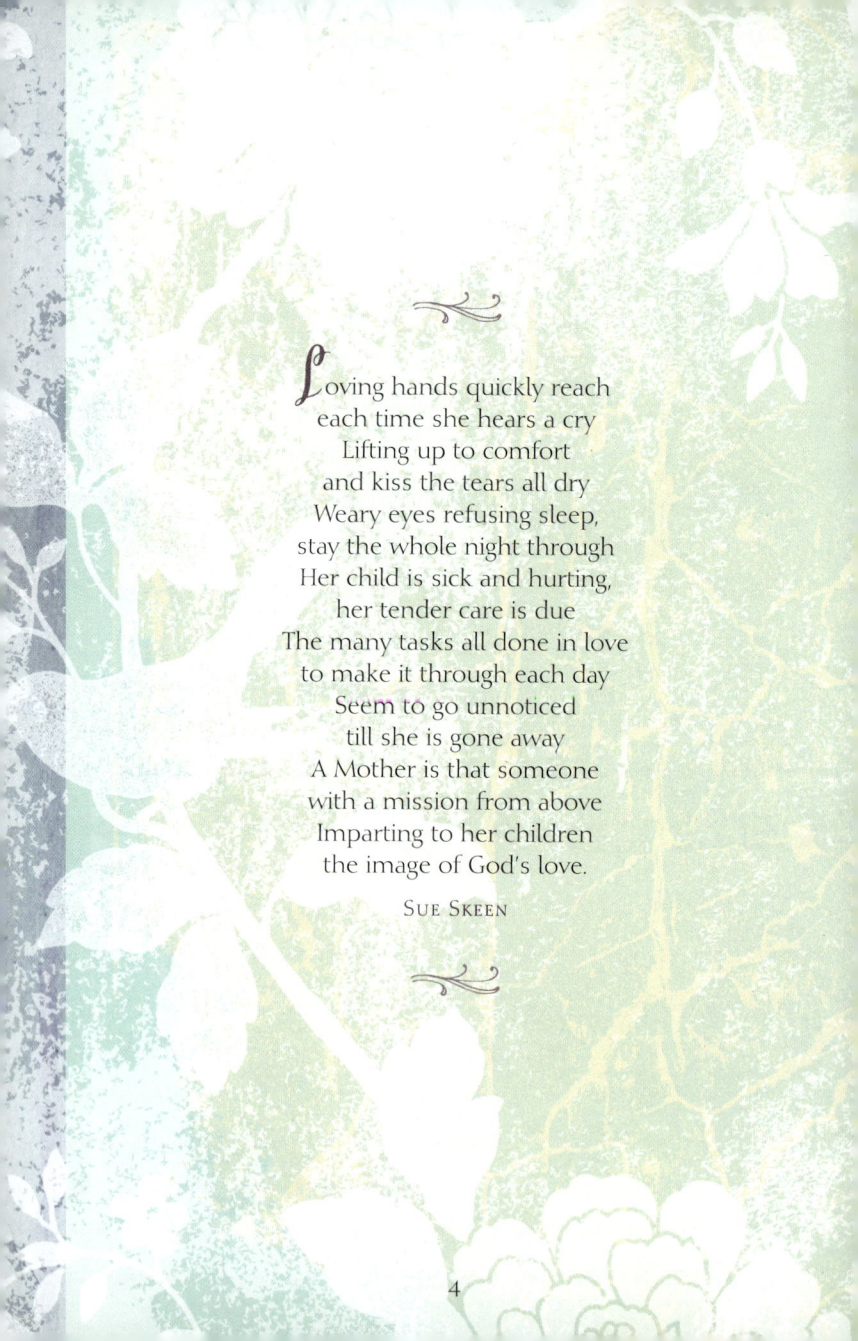

Loving hands quickly reach
each time she hears a cry
Lifting up to comfort
and kiss the tears all dry
Weary eyes refusing sleep,
stay the whole night through
Her child is sick and hurting,
her tender care is due
The many tasks all done in love
to make it through each day
Seem to go unnoticed
till she is gone away
A Mother is that someone
with a mission from above
Imparting to her children
the image of God's love.

SUE SKEEN

Experience God in the breathless wonder
and startling beauty that is all around you.
His sun shines warm upon your face.
His wind whispers in the treetops.
Like the first rays of morning light,
celebrate the start of each day with God.

Every good and perfect gift is from above, coming down from the Father.

JAMES 1:17 NIV

Gratitude unlocks the fullness of life.
It turns what we have into enough, and more....
It can turn a meal into a feast, a house
into a home, a stranger into a friend.
Gratitude makes sense of our past, brings peace
for today, and creates a vision for tomorrow.

MELODY BEATTIE

God Bless You

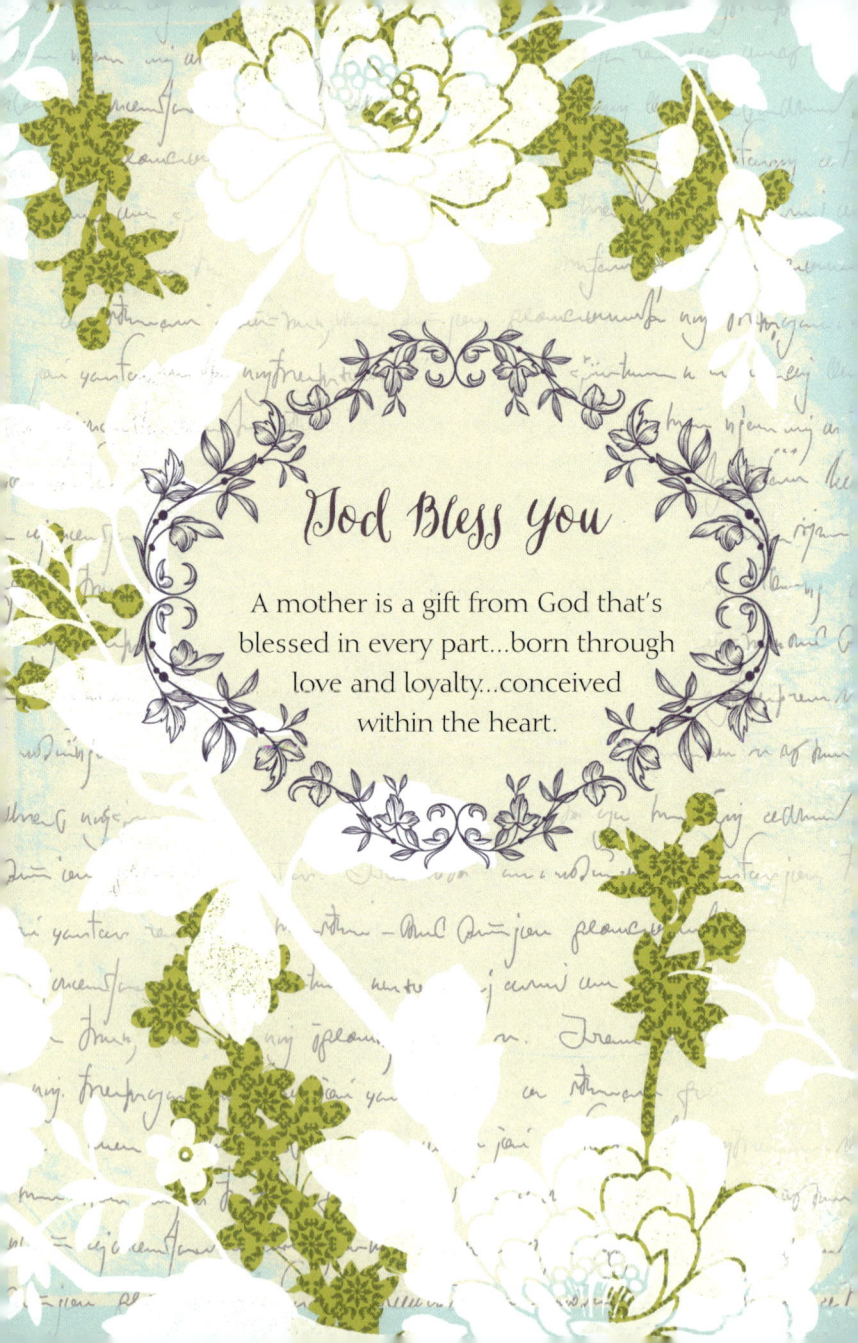

A mother is a gift from God that's blessed in every part...born through love and loyalty...conceived within the heart.

Parents who instruct and nurture their children in God's ways will see fulfilled that great promise—"he will not depart from it."

CATHERINE MARSHALL

~

I call to remembrance the genuine faith that is in you, which dwelt first in your grandmother Lois and your mother Eunice, and I am persuaded is in you also.

2 TIMOTHY 1:5 NKJV

~

As the chaos swirls and life's demands pull at me on all sides, I will breathe in God's peace that surpasses all understanding. He has promised that He would set within me a peace too deeply planted to be affected by unexpected or exhausting demands.

A mom's hug lasts long after she lets go

~

Each day is a treasure box of gifts from God, just waiting to be opened. Open your gifts with excitement. You will find forgiveness attached to ribbons of joy. You will find love wrapped in sparkling gems.

JOAN CLAYTON

~

I will bless you, and make your name great; and you shall be a blessing.

GENESIS 12:2 NASB

~

Being a mother means that your heart is no longer yours; it wanders wherever your children do.

*Youth fades; love droops;
the leaves of friendship fall;
a mother's secret hope outlives them all.*

OLIVER WENDELL HOLMES

Lift up your eyes. Your heavenly Father waits to bless you—in inconceivable ways to make your life what you never dreamed it could be.

ANNE ORTLUND

---

*May the LORD, the God of your ancestors,
multiply you a thousand times
and bless you as he promised!*

DEUTERONOMY 1:11 NLT

*Bless our children, God, and help us so
to fashion their souls by precept and example
that they may ever love the good, flee from sin,
revere Thy Word, and honor Thy name.*

UNION PRAYER BOOK

*God has not promised sun without rain,
joy without sorrow, peace without pain.
But God has promised strength for the day,
rest for the labor, light for the way,
grace for the trials, help from above,
unfailing sympathy, undying love.*

ANNIE JOHNSON FLINT

$\mathcal{I}$ wish I had a box, the biggest I could find, I'd fill it right up to the brim with everything that's kind. A box without a lock, of course, and never any key; for everything inside that box would then be offered free. Grateful words for joys received I'd freely give away. Oh, let us open wide a box of praise for every day.

*Her children arise and call her blessed;
her husband also, and he praises her:
"Many women do noble things,
but you surpass them all."*

PROVERBS 31:28–29 NIV

The Beauty of Life

To be a child is to know the joy of living. To have a child is to know the beauty of life.

Most of all the other beautiful things
in life come by twos and threes, by dozens
and hundreds. Plenty of roses, stars, sunsets,
rainbows, brothers and sisters, aunts and cousins,
comrades and friends—but only one
mother in the whole world.

KATE DOUGLAS WIGGIN

Something deep in all of us yearns
for God's beauty, and we can find
it no matter where we are.

SUE MONK KIDD

God has made everything beautiful
for its own time. He has planted eternity
in the human heart.

ECCLESIASTES 3:11 NLT

*You are God's created beauty
and the focus of His
affection and delight.*

JANET WEAVER SMITH

~~~

We are so busy in our lives that we need to purposely give attention to the everyday things that can make our lives lovelier, such as keeping a vase of fresh flowers in an obvious place, or several places in the house. Planting roses or other flowers for this purpose makes sense.

EMILIE BARNES

~~~

Therefore, as God's chosen people, holy and dearly loved, clothe yourselves with compassion, kindness, humility, gentleness and patience.

COLOSSIANS 3:12 NIV

*Today a new sun rises for me;
everything lives, everything is animated,
everything seems to speak to me of my passion,
everything invites me to cherish it.*

ANNE DE LENCLOS

---

*Consider the lilies, how they grow: they neither
toil nor spin; and yet I say to you, even Solomon
in all his glory was not arrayed like one of these.
If then God so clothes the grass, which today is in
the field and tomorrow is thrown into the oven,
how much more will he clothe you?*

LUKE 12:27–28 NKJV

---

*For attractive lips, speak words of kindness.
For lovely eyes, seek out the good in people.
For a slim figure, share your food with the hungry.
For beautiful hair, let a child run his or her fingers
through it once a day. For poise, walk with the
knowledge you'll never walk alone.*

AUDREY HEPBURN

$\mathcal{B}$eauty puts a face on God. When we gaze
at nature, at a loved one, at a work of art,
our soul immediately recognizes
and is drawn to the face of God.

MARGARET BROWNLEY

*May God give you eyes to see beauty
only the heart can understand.
Every time you smile at someone,
it is an action of love,
a gift to that person, a beautiful thing.*

MOTHER TERESA

$\mathcal{L}$ORD, you alone are my inheritance,
my cup of blessing. You guard all that is mine.
The land you have given me is a pleasant land.
What a wonderful inheritance!

PSALM 16:5-6 NLT

Isn't it a wonderful morning? The world looks like something God had just imagined for His own pleasure.

LUCY MAUD MONTGOMERY

Let there be many windows in your soul, that all the glory of the universe may beautify it.

ELLA WHEELER WILCOX

As God's workmanship, we deserve to be treated, and to treat ourselves, with affection and affirmation, regardless of our appearance or performance.

MARY ANN MAYO

In all ranks of life the human heart yearns for the beautiful, and the beautiful things that God makes are His gift to all alike.

HARRIET BEECHER STOWE

The Gift of Simplicity

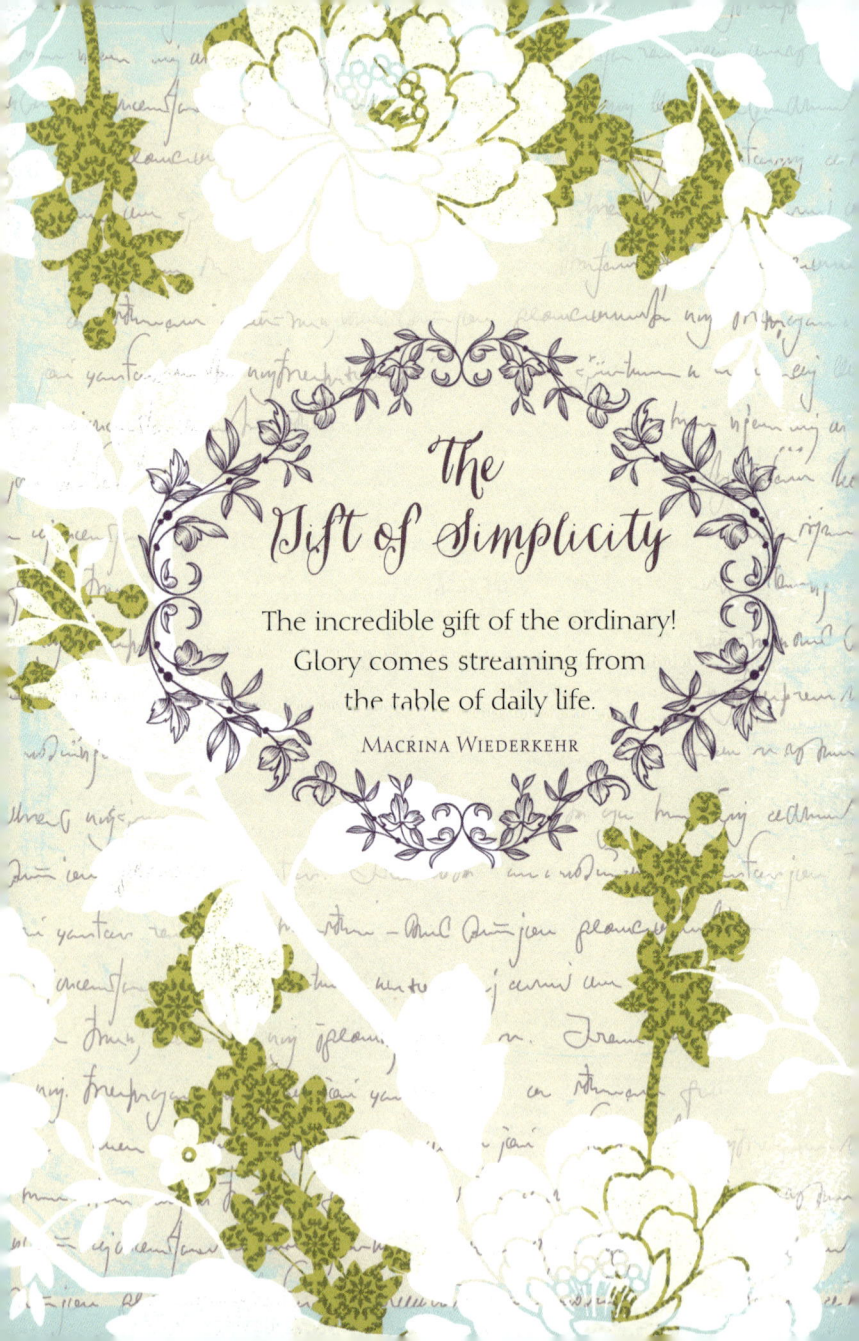

The incredible gift of the ordinary!
Glory comes streaming from
the table of daily life.

MACRINA WIEDERKEHR

My childhood home was the home of a woman with a genius for inventing daily life, who found happiness in the simplest of gestures.

LAURA FRONTY

Happy people...enjoy the fundamental, often very simple things of life.... They savor the moment, glad to be alive, enjoying their work, their families, the good things around them. They are adaptable; they can bend with the wind, adjust to the changes in their times, enjoy the contest of life.... Their eyes are turned outward; they are aware, compassionate. They have the capacity to love.

JANE CANFIELD

Let us consider how we may spur one another on toward love and good deeds, not giving up meeting together, as some are in the habit of doing, but encouraging one another.

HEBREWS 10:24–25 NIV

*E*njoy the little things. One day you may look back and realize…they were the big things.

※

*I*t doesn't take monumental feats to make the world a better place. It can be as simple as letting someone go ahead of you in a grocery line.

BARBARA JOHNSON

※

*N*ot every day of our lives is overflowing with joy and celebration. But there are moments when our hearts nearly burst within us for the sheer joy of being alive. The first sight of our newborn babies, the warmth of love in another's eyes, the fresh scent of rain on a hot summer's eve—moments like these renew in us a heartfelt appreciation for life.

GWEN ELLIS

*He leads the humble in justice,
and He teaches the humble His way.*

PSALM 25:9 NASB

※

With our children who thrive on simple pleasures, our work and our entire society can be renewed.

SARA WENGER SHENK

※

Don't ever let yourself get so busy that you
miss those little but important extras in life—
the beauty of a day, the smile of a friend,
the serenity of a quiet moment alone.
For it is often life's smallest pleasures
and gentlest joys that make the biggest
and most lasting difference.

A fiery sunset, tiny pansies by the wayside, the sound of raindrops tapping on the roof—what extraordinary delight we find in the simple wonders of life! With wide eyes and full hearts, we may cherish what others often miss.

A devout life does bring wealth, but it's the rich simplicity of being yourself before God. Since we entered the world penniless and will leave it penniless, if we have bread on the table and shoes on our feet, that's enough.

1 TIMOTHY 6:6 MSG

It isn't the great big pleasures that count the most; it's making a great deal out of the little ones.

JEAN WEBSTER

It is the little things that count
And give a mother pleasure—
The things her children bring to her
Which they so richly treasure...
The picture that is smudged a bit
With tiny fingerprints,
The colored rock, the lightning bugs,
The sticky peppermints;
The ragged, bright bouquet of flowers
A child brings, roots and all—
These things delight a mother's heart
Although they seem quite small.
A mother can see beauty
In the very smallest thing
For there's a little bit of heaven
In a small child's offering.

KATHERINE NELSON DAVIS

My Heart Is Content

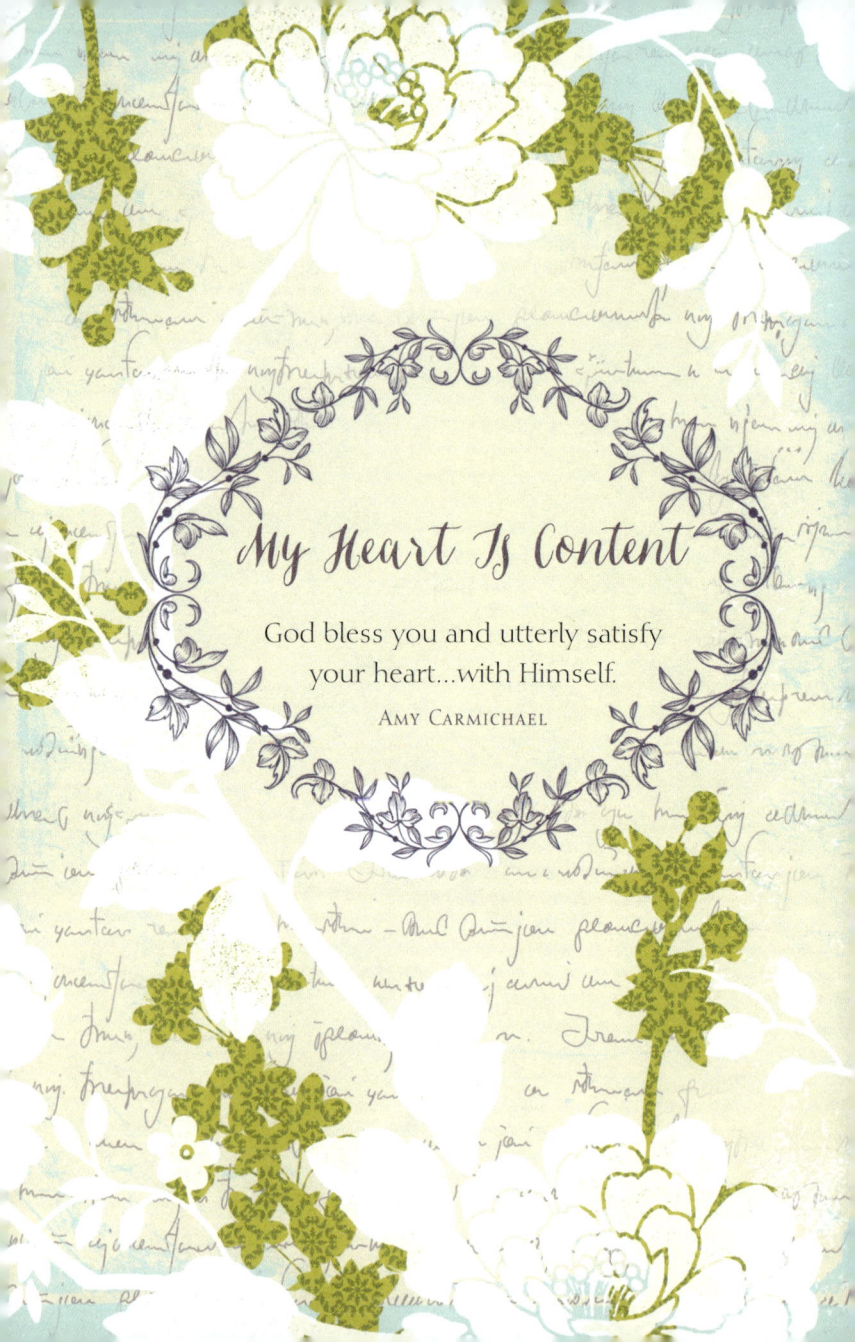

God bless you and utterly satisfy
your heart...with Himself.

Amy Carmichael

*It is always wise to stop wishing
for things long enough to enjoy the fragrance
of those now flowering.*

PATRICE GIFFORD

---

*Children have neither past nor future;
they enjoy the present,
which very few of us do.*

JEAN DE LA BRUYÉRE

---

*I have learned how to be content (satisfied to
the point where I am not disturbed or disquieted)
in whatever state I am.... I have learned in any
and all circumstances the secret of facing every
situation, whether well-fed or going hungry,
having a sufficiency and enough to spare
or going without and being in want.*

PHILIPPIANS 4:11–12 AMP

*Life is not intended to be simply a round
of work, no matter how interesting
and important that work may be. A moment's
pause to watch the glory of a sunrise or a sunset
is soul satisfying, while a bird's song will set
the steps to music all day long.*

Laura Ingalls Wilder

*Where the soul is full of peace and joy, outward
surroundings and circumstances
are of comparatively little account.*

Hannah Whitall Smith

*My heart is content with just knowing
fulfillment that true friendship brings;
it fills to the brim, overflowing with pleasure
in life's "little things."*

June Masters Bacher

Be still, and know that I am God.

PSALM 46:10 NKJV

Women of adventure have conquered their fates and know how to live exciting and fulfilling lives right where they are. They have learned to reinvent themselves and find creative ways to enjoy the world and their place in it. They know how to take mini-vacations, stop and smell the roses, and live fully in the moment.

BARBARA JENKINS

Let the day suffice, with all its joys and failings, its little triumphs and defeats.... Happily, if sleepily, welcome evening as a time of rest, and let it slip away, losing nothing.

KATHLEEN NORRIS

When we put people before possessions
in our hearts, we are sowing seeds
of enduring satisfaction.

Beverly LaHaye

I am still determined to be cheerful and happy, in whatever situation I may be; for I have also learned from experience that the greater part of our happiness or misery depends upon our dispositions, and not upon our circumstances.

Martha Washington

We brought nothing into
this world, and it is certain
we can carry nothing out.
And having food and clothing,
with these we shall be content.

1 Timothy 6:7–8 nkjv

God is helping me to be content to set certain gifts on the shelf at present for the sake of my family. He is teaching me that He is more interested in what I am than in what I do.

Sandra K. Strubhar

Normal day, let me be aware of the treasure you are. Let me learn from you, love you, bless you before you depart. Let me not pass you by in quest of some rare and perfect tomorrow.

Everything has its wonders, even darkness and silence, and I learn, whatever state I may be in, herein to be content.

Helen Keller

Contentment is not the fulfillment of what you want, but the realization of how much you already have.

The Richness of Friendship

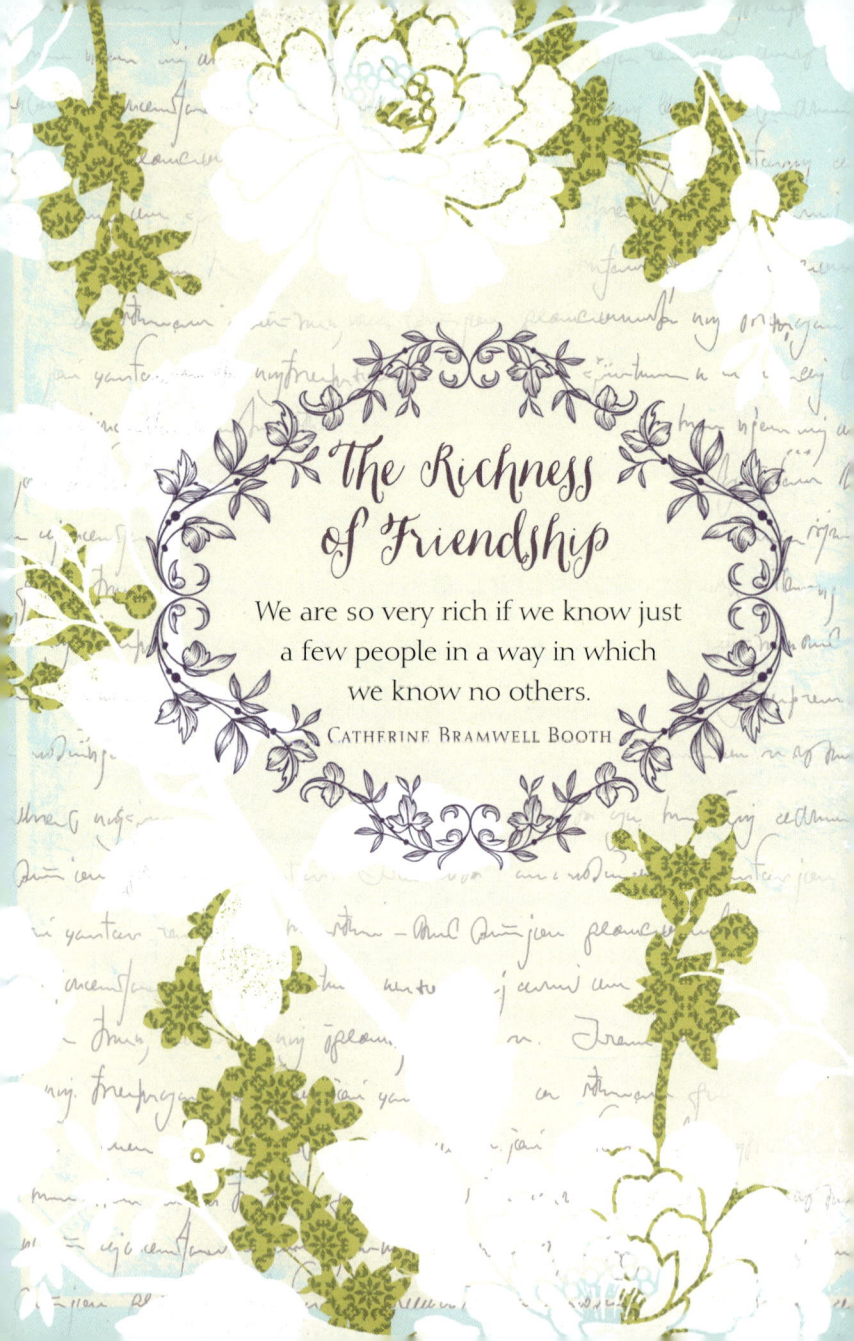

We are so very rich if we know just a few people in a way in which we know no others.

CATHERINE BRAMWELL BOOTH

Knowing what to say is not always necessary; just the presence of a caring friend can make a world of difference.

SHERI CURRY

Our ancient female ancestors walked to wells and rivers together to get water. Our great grandmothers quilted and canned together. We, instead, are imprisoned in our minivans driving breakneck speed, thinking a few maniacal minutes on a cell phone can replace a regular play-date where believing moms can take some time to laugh and share. I don't think it's a luxury. It's a necessity for mental (and often spiritual!) health!

BETH MOORE

Friends love through all kinds of weather, and families stick together in all kinds of trouble.

PROVERBS 17:17 MSG

If we would build on a sure foundation in friendship, we must love friends for their sake rather than for our own.

CHARLOTTE BRONTË

Oh, the comfort, the inexpressible comfort of feeling safe with a person—having neither to weigh thoughts nor measure words, but pouring them all right out just as they are, chaff and grain together, certain that a faithful hand will take and sift them, keep what is worth keeping and then, with the breath of kindness, blow the rest away.

DINAH MARIA MULOCK CRAIK

Stay true to the Lord. I love you and long to see you, dear friends, for you are my joy.

PHILIPPIANS 4:1 NLT

Don't walk in front of me—I may not follow. Don't walk behind me—I may not lead. Walk beside me—and just be my friend.

Having someone who understands is a great blessing for ourselves. Being someone who understands is a great blessing to others.

JANETTE OKE

Friendship is the fruit gathered from the trees planted in the rich soil of love, and nurtured with tender care and understanding.

ALMA L. WEIXELBAUM

We should all have one person who knows how to bless us despite the evidence.

PHYLLIS THEROUX

Treat your friends like family and your family like friends. Everyone was meant to share God's all-abiding love and care; He saw that we would need to know a way to let these feelings show.... So God made hugs.

JILL WOLF

Insomuch as any one pushes you nearer to God, he or she is your friend.

FRENCH PROVERB

I am only as strong as the coffee I drink, the hairspray I use, and the friends I have.

The Lord confides in those who fear him;
he makes his covenant known to them.

PSALM 25:14 NIV

Good communication is stimulating
as black coffee, and just as hard to sleep after.

ANNE MORROW LINDBERGH

A friend understands what you are trying
to say...even when your thoughts
aren't fitting into words.

ANN D. PARRISH

A friend hears the song in my heart
and sings it to me when my memory fails.

Listening...means taking a vigorous, human
interest in what is being told us. You can listen like
a blank wall or like a splendid auditorium where
every sound comes back fuller and richer.

ALICE DUER MILLER

Providing All Our Needs

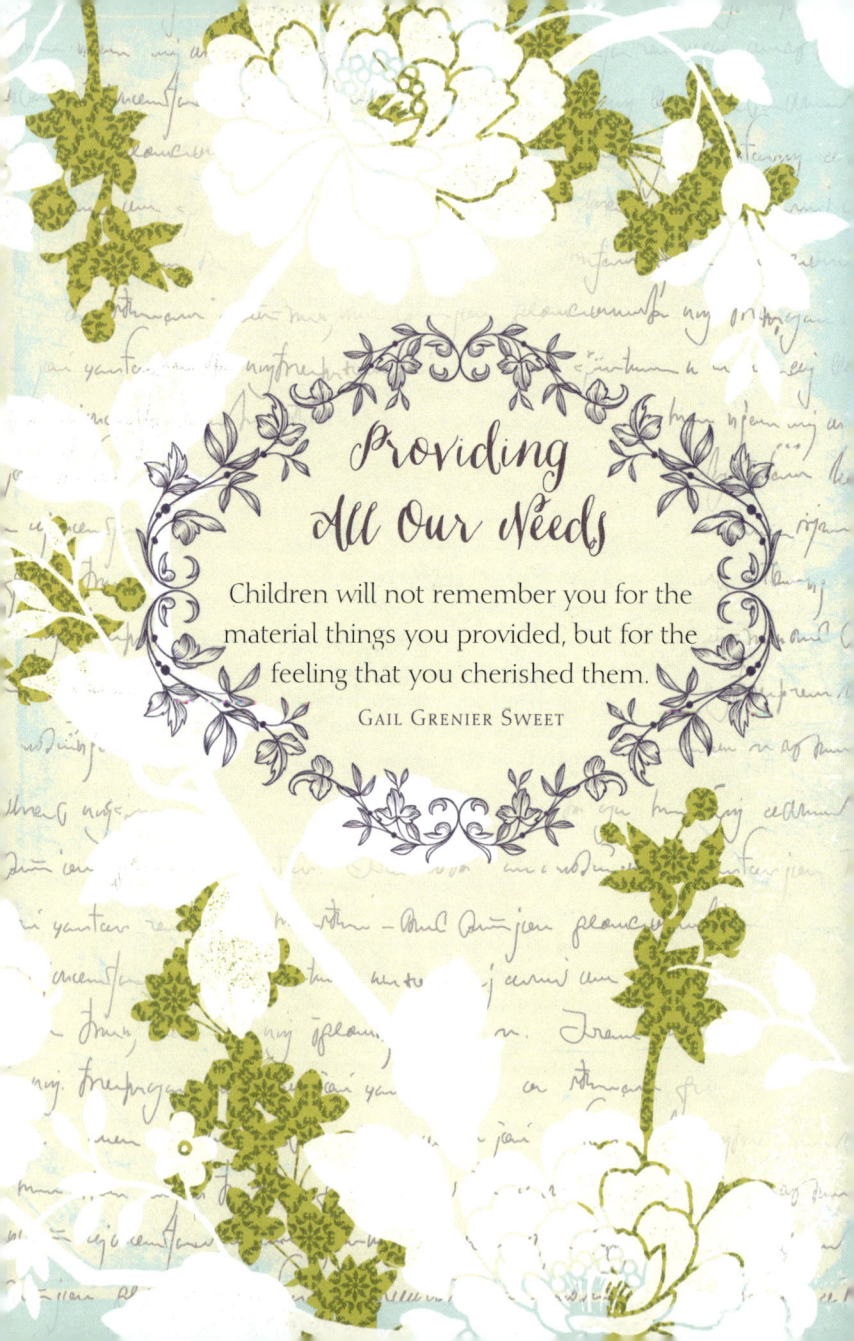

Children will not remember you for the material things you provided, but for the feeling that you cherished them.

GAIL GRENIER SWEET

*I must simply be thankful,
and I am, for all the Lord
has provided for me, whether big
or small in the eyes of someone else.*

MABEL P. ADAMSON

She is their earth.... She is their food and their bed and the extra blanket when it grows cold in the night; she is their warmth and their health and their shelter.

KATHERINE BUTLER HATHAWAY

They might not need me; but they might. I'll let my head be just in sight; a smile as small as mine might be precisely their necessity.

EMILY DICKINSON

You can trust God right now to supply all your needs for today. And if your needs are more tomorrow, His supply will be greater also.

*It is not my business
to think about myself.
My business is to think about God.
It is for God to think about me.*

SIMONE WEIL

My God will liberally supply (fill to the full) your every need according to His riches in glory in Christ Jesus.

PHILIPPIANS 4:19 AMP

Give me understanding according to Your word.

PSALM 119:169 NASB

~

The very word "motherhood" has
an emotional depth and significance
few terms have. It bespeaks nourishment
and safety and sheltering arms.

MARJORIE HOLMES

~

Those who know God as their Father know
the whole secret. They are His heirs,
and may enter now into possession of all
that is necessary for their present needs.

HANNAH WHITALL SMITH

~

Throughout the Bible, when God asked someone
to do something, methods, means, materials,
and specific directions were always provided.
That person had one thing to do: obey.

ELISABETH ELLIOT

You care for the land and water it; you enrich it abundantly. The streams of God are filled with water to provide the people with grain, for so you have ordained it.

PSALM 65:9 NIV

God's gifts make us truly wealthy. His loving supply never shall leave us wanting.

BECKY LAIRD

There will be days which are great and everything goes as planned. There will be other days when we aren't sure why we got out of bed. Regardless of which kind of day it is, we can be assured that God takes care of our daily needs.

EMILIE BARNES

A mother is a person who, seeing there are only four pieces of pie for five people, promptly announces she never did care for pie.

TENNEVA JORDAN

If you have a special need today, focus your full attention on the goodness and greatness of your Father rather than on the size of your need. Your need is so small compared to His ability to meet it.

Tradition is a form of promise from parent to child. It's a way to say, "I love you," "I'm here for you," and "Some things will not change."

LYNN LUDWICK

Wisdom to Live By

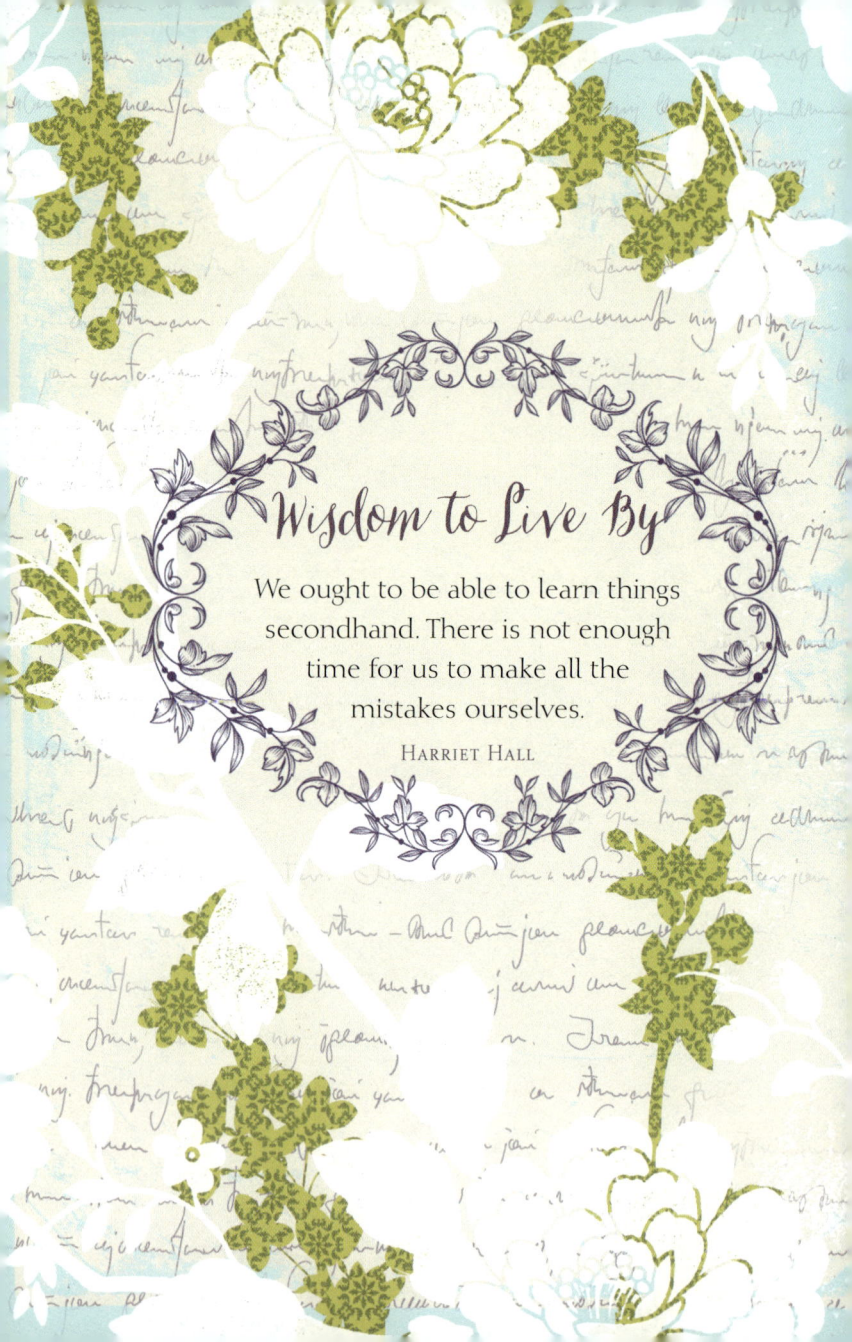

We ought to be able to learn things secondhand. There is not enough time for us to make all the mistakes ourselves.

HARRIET HALL

*Those who came before us
will teach you. They will teach
you the wisdom of old.*

JOB 8:10 NLT

~~~

Heavenly Father, please give me wisdom
in daily protecting my children.
Whether it's concerning the people they
come in contact with, the television
and videos they watch, or the many
other issues that affect them,
may I be aware of my responsibility to guide
and nurture their minds. Amen.

KIM BOYCE

~~~

Women can do no greater thing than to create
the climate of love in their homes. Love which
spoils and pampers, weakens and hampers.
Real love strengthens and matures and leaves
the loved one free to grow.

EUGENIA PRICE

I am convinced beyond a shadow of any doubt that the most valuable pursuit we can embark upon is to know God.

KAY ARTHUR

Wisdom is knowing the truth, and telling it.

Having three children in three years was a great pruning experience in my life. It was God's creative way of putting me in a situation where I had to learn patience.

CYNTHIA HEALD

Children require guidance and sympathy far more than instruction.

ANNE SULLIVAN

At the end of your life you will never regret not having passed one more test, not winning one more verdict, or not closing one more deal. You will regret time not spent with a husband, a friend, a child, or a parent.

BARBARA BUSH

―――

As for the days of our life, they contain seventy years, or if due to strength, eighty years…. Soon it is gone and we fly away…. So teach us to number our days, that we may present to You a heart of wisdom.

PSALM 90:10, 12 NASB

―――

Whenever I need help being a mother, I remember my mother and grandmother, women who planted seeds of wisdom in my soul, like a secret garden, to flower even in the bitterest cold.

JUDITH TOWSE-ROBERTS

With Him are wisdom and strength,
He has counsel and understanding.

JOB 12:13 NKJV

All things bright and beautiful,
All creatures great and small,
All things wise and wonderful,
The Lord God made them all.

CECIL FRANCES ALEXANDER

A child's hand in yours—what tenderness
and power it arouses. You are instantly
the very touchstone of wisdom and strength.

MARJORIE HOLMES

The mother's heart is the child's school-room.

HENRY WARD BEECHER

A wise gardener plants his seeds,
then has the good sense not to dig them
up every few days to see if a crop is on the way.
Likewise, we must be patient as God brings
the answers...in His own good time.

QUIN SHERRER

For the wisdom of the wisest being God has made ends in wonder; and there is nothing on earth so wonderful as the budding soul of a little child.

LUCY LARCOM

Love does not delight in evil but rejoices with the truth. It always protects, always trusts, always hopes, always perseveres. Love never fails.

1 CORINTHIANS 13:6–8 NIV

Covering of Prayer

When we call on God, He bends down
His ear to listen, as a father bends down
to listen to his little child.

ELIZABETH CHARLES

When you were small and just a touch away,
I covered you with blankets against the cool night air.
But now that you are tall and out of reach,
I fold my hands and cover you with prayer.

DONA MADDUX COOPER

---

*To live in prayer together
is to walk in love together.*

MARGARET MOORE JACOBS

Snowflakes are one of nature's most
fragile things, but just look what they
can do when they stick together.

VESTA M. KELLY

On the day I called, You answer me;
You made me bold with strength in my soul.

PSALM 138:3 NASB

*O*pen wide the windows of our spirits and fill us full of light; open wide the door of our hearts that we may receive and entertain Thee with all the powers of our adoration.

CHRISTINA ROSSETTI

---

*W*hen we pray, our children learn they are welcome in God's presence, and they become confident in going to Him. As praying mothers, we not only *let* our children come to Him, we *lead* them to Him for life.

BONNIE JENSEN

I cannot begin to express to You how greatly blessed and grateful I am for the gift of my children. I do, with all my heart, receive each life that has come into our family as Your beautiful gift. I cannot find the words to thank You enough.

ROY LESSIN

Rejoice always; pray without ceasing; in everything give thanks; for this is God's will for you in Christ Jesus.

1 Thessalonians 5:16–18 NASB

I said a prayer for you today
And I know God must have heard,
I felt the answer in my heart
Although He spoke no word.
I asked that He'd be near you
At the start of each new day,
To grant you health and blessings
And friends to share the way.
I asked for happiness for you
In all things great and small,
But it was His loving care
I prayed for most of all.

We must take our troubles to the Lord,
but we must do more than that;
we must leave them there.

HANNAH WHITALL SMITH

Whate'er the care which breaks thy rest,
Whate'er the wish that swells thy breast;
Spread before God that wish, that care,
And change anxiety to prayer.

Lord, thank You for my children. Please inspire
me with ways to show them my love and Yours.
I want them to feel appreciated. I want to help
and encourage them.... I want to bless them.

QUIN SHERRER

Whoever does not receive the kingdom of God
as a little child will by no means enter it."
And He took them up in His arms, laid His hands
on them, and blessed them.

MARK 10:15–16 NKJV

Allow your dreams a place in your prayers and plans. God-given dreams can help you move into the future He is preparing for you.

BARBARA JOHNSON

You pay God a compliment by asking great things of Him.

TERESA OF AVILA

Be kindly affectionate to one another...fervent in spirit, serving the Lord; rejoicing in hope, patient in tribulation, continuing steadfastly in prayer; distributing to the needs of the saints, given to hospitality.

ROMANS 12:10–13 NKJV

It is when things go wrong, when good things do not happen, when our prayers seem to have been lost, that God is most present.

MADELEINE L'ENGLE

A Mother's Influence

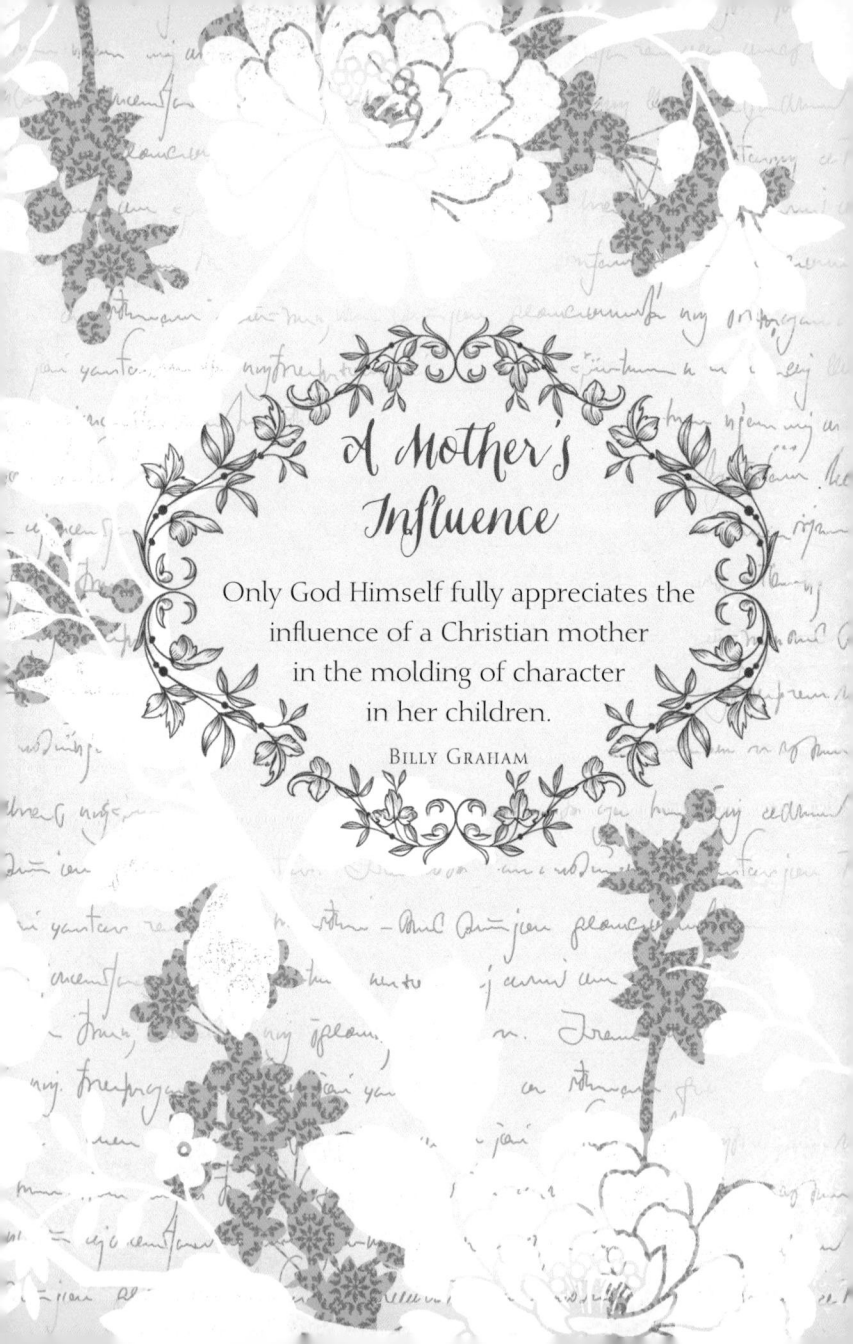

Only God Himself fully appreciates the
influence of a Christian mother
in the molding of character
in her children.

BILLY GRAHAM

The fullness of our heart is expressed
in our eyes, in our touch, in what we write,
in what we say, in the way we walk, the way
we receive, the way we need.

Mother Teresa

---

*The best thing that you can give
your children, next to good habits,
is good memories.*

Barbara Johnson

How blessed the man you train, God,
the woman you instruct in your Word,
providing a circle of quiet within the clamor
of evil.... God will never walk away from
his people, never desert his precious people.
Rest assured that justice is on its way
and every good heart put right.

Psalm 94:12–15 msg

God, help me to be honest so my children will learn honesty. Help me to be kind so my children will learn kindness. Help me to be faithful so my children will learn faith. Help me to love so that my children will be loving.

MARIAN WRIGHT EDELMAN

Train up a child in the way he should go [and in keeping with his individual gift or bent], and when he is old he will not depart from it.

PROVERBS 22:6 AMP

Instant availability without continuous presence is probably the best role a mother can play.

L. BAILY

There is no influence so powerful as that of the mother.

SARAH JOSEPHA HALE

―≾―

The blossom cannot tell what becomes of its fragrance as it drifts away, just as no person can tell what becomes of her influence as she continues through life.

―≾―

There is nothing higher and stronger and more wholesome and useful for life in later years than some good memory, especially a memory connected with childhood, with home. If a person carries many such memories with them into life, they are safe to the end of their days, and if we have only one good memory left in our hearts, even that may sometime be the means of saving us.

FYODOR DOSTOYEVSKY

Whether we are poets or parents or teachers or artists or gardeners, we must start where we are and use what we have. In the process of creation and relationship, what seems mundane and trivial may show itself to be holy, precious, part of a pattern.

LUCI SHAW

To discipline a child produces wisdom.... Discipline your children, and they will give you peace of mind and will make your heart glad.

PROVERBS 29:15, 17 NLT

An ounce of mother is worth a pound of clergy.

RUDYARD KIPLING

The most important thing she'd learned over
the years was that there was no way to be a perfect
mother and a million ways to be a good one.

Jill Churchill

Kindness is the only service that will stand
the storm of life and not wash out. It will
wear well and be remembered long after
the prism of politeness or the complexion
of courtesy has faded away.

May the beauty of Your Spirit be so evident
in me that I will be a godly role model. Give me
the communication, teaching, and nurturing skills
that I must have. Make me the parent You want
me to be and teach me how to pray and truly
intercede for the life of this child.

Stormie Omartian

Taking Time to Love

Dear Lord, please help me to remember to take the time to bestow the kisses today that I want loved ones to remember tomorrow.

JENNIFER THOMAS

Make the most of every opportunity. Let your conversation be gracious and attractive so that you will have the right response for everyone.

COLOSSIANS 4:5–6 NLT

Mama's order was heavenly. It had to do with thoroughness...and taking plenty of time. It had to do with taking plenty of time with me.

SUSANNAH LESSARD

Getting things accomplished isn't nearly as important as taking time for love.

JANETTE OKE

Live each day the fullest you can, not guaranteeing there'll be a tomorrow, not dwelling endlessly on yesterday.

JANE SEYMOUR

Be still, and in the quiet moments,
listen to the voice of your heavenly Father.
His words can renew your spirit.... No one knows
you and your needs like He does.

JANET WEAVER SMITH

---

*Blessed is the person who is too busy
to worry in the daytime
and too sleepy to worry at night.*

CAROLINE SCHROEDER

Forgetting those things which are behind
and reaching forward to those things which are
ahead, I press toward the goal for the prize
of the upward call of God in Christ Jesus.

PHILIPPIANS 3:13–14 NKJV

Can you measure the worth of a sunbeam,
The worth of a treasured smile,
The value of love and of giving,
The things that make life worthwhile?...
Can you measure the value of friendship,
Of knowing that someone is there,
Of faith and of hope and of courage,
A treasured and goodly share?
For nothing is higher in value,
Whatever life chooses to send—
We must prove that we, too, are worthy
And equal the worth of a friend.

GARNETT ANN SCHULTZ

We must not, in trying to think about how we can make a big difference, ignore the small daily differences we can make which, over time, add up to big differences that we often cannot foresee.

MARIAN WRIGHT EDELMAN

Take time to notice all the usually unnoticed, simple things in life. Delight in the never-ending hope that's available every day!

***

Choices can change our lives profoundly. The choice to mend a broken relationship, to say yes to a difficult assignment, to lay aside some important work to play with a child, to visit some forgotten person—these small choices may affect our lives eternally.

GLORIA GAITHER

***

Time is a very precious gift of God; so precious that it's only given to us moment by moment.

AMELIA BARR

Just accept the fact that as long
as you have children in your home,
your house is going to get messy.

LISA WHELCHEL

The generous will themselves be blessed,
for they share their food with the poor.

PROVERBS 22:9 NIV

See each morning a world made anew,
as if it were the morning of the very first day...
treasure and use it, as if it were the final hour
of the very last day.

FAY HARTZELL ARNOLD

True worth is in being, not seeming—in doing,
each day that goes by, some little good—not in
dreaming of great things to do by and by.

ALICE CARY

God Our Father

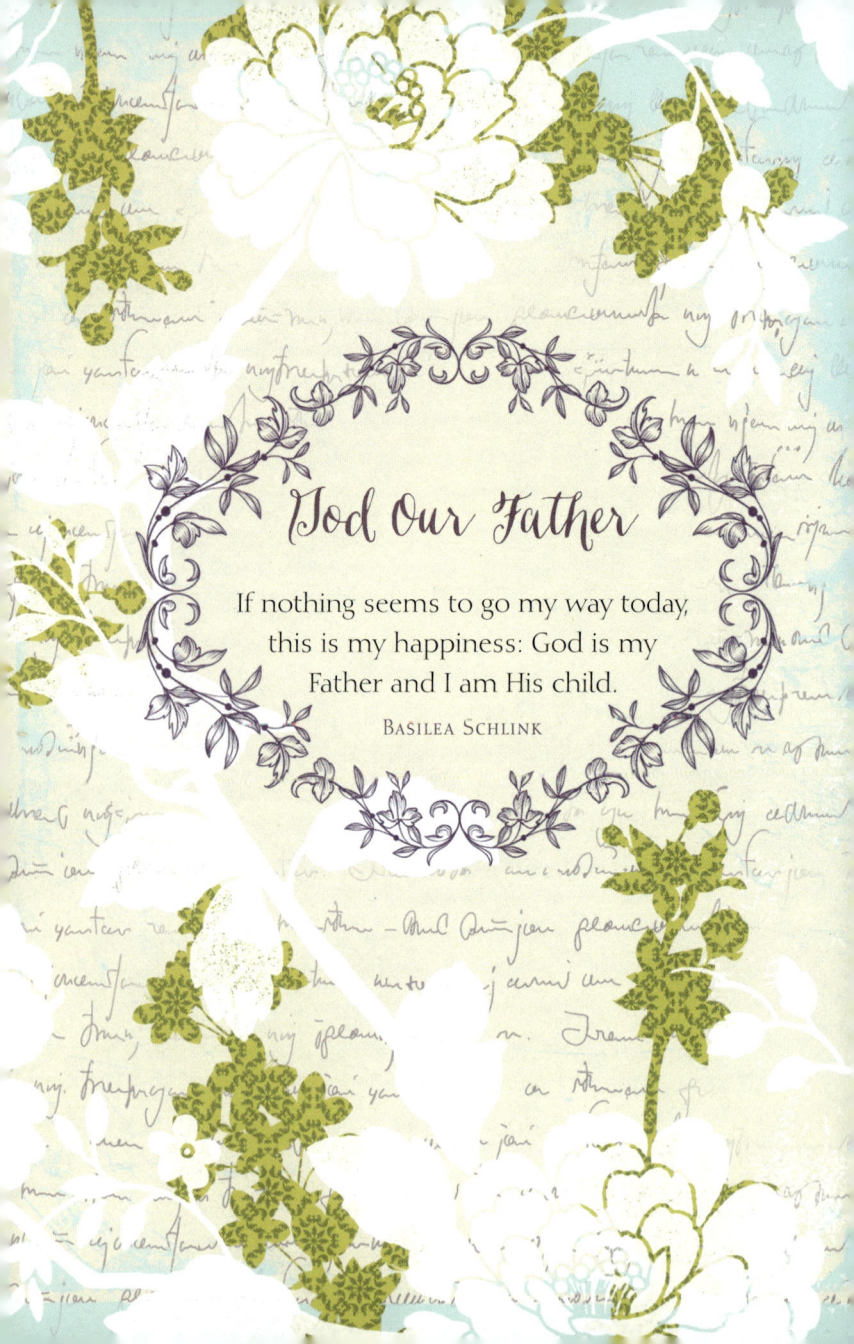

If nothing seems to go my way today,
this is my happiness: God is my
Father and I am His child.

BASILEA SCHLINK

As a rose fills a room with its fragrance,
so will God's love fill our lives.

MARGARET BROWNLEY

God is every moment totally aware of each one of us. Totally aware in intense concentration and love.... No one passes through any area of life, happy or tragic, without the attention of God.

EUGENIA PRICE

For my dear little child I'd lasso the moon
and give you my love on a silver spoon.
I'd run 'round the world and back again, too,
to grant you the hope of days bright and new.
But all that I have and all that I do is nothing
compared to God's love for you.

Whoever walks toward God one step,
God runs toward him two.

JEWISH PROVERB

I wanted nothing more than to give you this beautiful land—the finest possession in the world. I looked forward to your calling me "Father," and I wanted you never to turn from me.

JEREMIAH 3:19 NLT

After the love of God, a mother's affection is the greatest treasure here below.

Children of the heavenly Father
Safely in His bosom gather;
Nestling bird nor star in heaven
Such a refuge e'er was given.

CAROLINA SANDELL BERG

Grace and peace to you from God
our Father and from the Lord Jesus Christ.

ROMANS 1:7 NIV

The treasure our heart searches for is found
in the ocean of God's love.

JANET WEAVER SMITH

Before anything else, above all else,
beyond everything else, God loves us.
God loves us extravagantly, ridiculously,
without limit or condition. God is in love
with us.... God yearns for us.

ROBERTA BONDI

My Father, You are the Lord my God.
I desire to love You, listen to Your voice,
and hold fast to You, for You, Lord, are my life.

BETH MOORE

Blue skies with white clouds on summer days.
A myriad of stars on clear moonlit nights.
Tulips and roses and violets and dandelions
and daisies. Bluebirds and laughter and sunshine
and Easter. See how He loves us!

ALICE CHAPIN

The God who created, names, and numbers
the stars in the heavens also numbers the hairs
of my head.… He pays attention to very big things
and to very small ones. What matters to me
matters to Him, and that changes my life.

ELISABETH ELLIOT

See what great the love the Father has lavished
on us, that we should be called children of God!
And that is what we are!

1 JOHN 3:1 NIV

God walks with us.... He scoops us up in His arms or simply sits with us in silent strength until we cannot avoid the awesome recognition that yes, even now, He is here.

GLORIA GAITHER

The Creator thinks enough of you to have sent Someone very special so that you might have life—abundantly, joyfully, completely, and victoriously. God is so big He can cover the whole world with His love, and so small He can curl up inside your heart.

JUNE MASTERS BACHER

Stand outside this evening. Look at the stars. Know that you are special and loved by the One who created them.

Thank You, Lord!

Thank You, Father, for loving all
the little children of the world—
no matter how old we are.

MARION BOND WEST

*Morning has broken like the first morning,
Blackbird has spoken like the first bird....
Praise with elation, praise every morning,
God's re-creation of the new day!*

ELEANOR FARJEON

---

*Every day shared with the ones
we love is a gift for which
we are very thankful!*

---

*Our thanksgiving today should include those
things which we take for granted, and we should
continually praise our God, who is true to His
promise, who has provided and retained
the necessities for our living.*

BETTY FUHRMAN

---

*He will feed His flock like a shepherd:
He will gather the lambs in His arm, He will
carry them in His bosom and will gently
lead those that have their young.*

ISAIAH 40:11 AMP

We Your people and the sheep of Your pasture will give thanks to You forever; to all generations we will tell of Your praise.

PSALM 79:13 NASB

May your life become one of glad and unending praise to the Lord as you journey through this world, and in the world that is to come!

TERESA OF AVILA

God desires that the work we do bring us enduring joy and satisfaction. This will naturally happen when our efforts are labors of love that bring Him glory and praise.

BEVERLY LaHAYE

Mothers are lots of things—doctors, writers, lawyers, gardeners, actresses, cooks, police officers, sometimes even truck drivers. And mothers. Thank You, Lord.

MADELEINE L'ENGLE

*Let's praise His name! He is holy,
He is almighty. He is love.
He brings hope, forgiveness,
heart cleansing, peace, and power.
He is our deliverer and coming King.
Praise His wonderful name!*

LUCILLE M. LAW

~~~

How much of our lives are...well...so daily.
How often our hours are filled with the mundane,
seemingly unimportant things that have to be
done, whether at home or work. These very "daily"
tasks could become a celebration of praise.
"It is through consecration," someone has said,
"that drudgery is made divine."

GIGI GRAHAM TCHIVIDJIAN

Thanksgiving puts power in living, because it opens the generators of the heart to respond gratefully, to receive joyfully, and to react creatively.

I have never committed the least matter to God, that I have not had reason for infinite praise.

ANNA SHIPTON

Thank God for dirty dishes;
They have a tale to tell.
While other folks go hungry,
We're eating pretty well.
With home, and health, and happiness,
We shouldn't want to fuss;
For by this stack of evidence,
God's very good to us.

Let us give all that lies within us...to pure praise, to pure loving adoration, and to worship from a grateful heart—a heart that is trained to look up.

AMY CARMICHAEL

God, of Your goodness give me Yourself, for You are enough for me. And only in You do I have everything.

JULIAN OF NORWICH

By Him, let us continually offer the sacrifice of praise to God, that is, the fruit of our lips, giving thanks to His name. But do not forget to do good and to share, for with such sacrifices God is well pleased.

HEBREWS 13:15–16 NKJV

Living in Truth

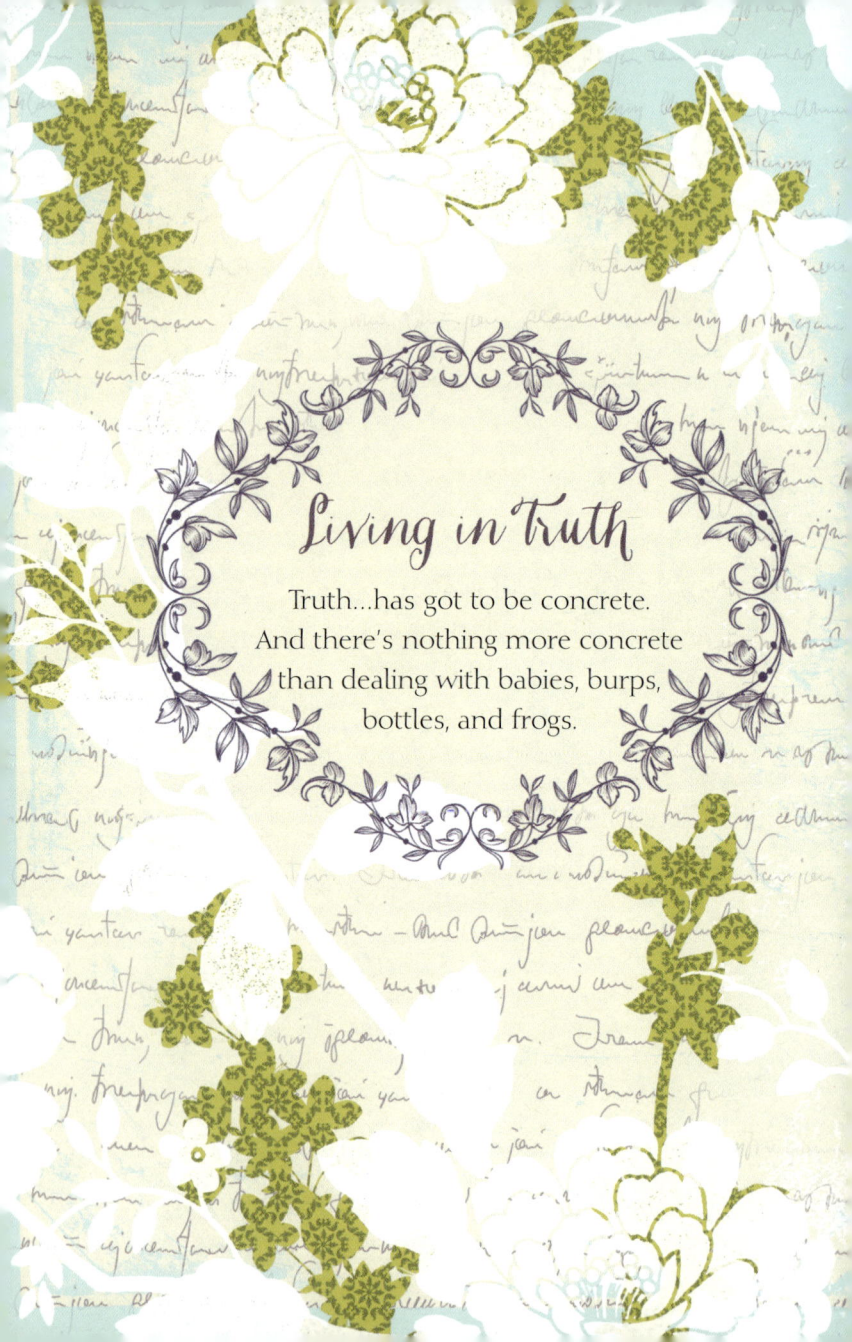

Truth…has got to be concrete.
And there's nothing more concrete
than dealing with babies, burps,
bottles, and frogs.

Truth is always exciting. Speak it, then. Life is dull without it.

PEARL S. BUCK

Anyone who examines this evidence
will come to stake his life on this:
that God himself is the truth.

JOHN 3:31 MSG

Amid ancient lore the Word of God stands
unique and pre-eminent. Wonderful in its
construction, admirable in its adaptation,
it contains truths that a child may comprehend,
and mysteries into which angels desire to look.

FRANCES ELLEN WATKINS HARPER

To follow truth as blind men long for light,
to do my best from dawn of day till night,
to keep my heart fit for His holy sight,
and answer when He calls. This is my task.

MAUDE LOUISE RAY

Jesus answered, "I am the way
and the truth and the life. No one comes
to the Father except through me."

JOHN 14:6 NIV

Truth-tellers are not always palatable.
There is a preference for candy bars.

GWENDOLYN BROOKS

There is no greater demonstration of God's
power to our children than when they see their
own parents receive answers to prayer.

QUIN SHERRER

Open my eyes that I may see
Glimpses of truth Thou hast for me.
Place in my hands the wonderful key
That shall unclasp and set me free:
Silently now I wait for Thee,
Ready, my God, Thy will to see;
Open my eyes, illumine me,
Spirit divine!

CLARA H. SCOTT

I am amazed by the sayings of Christ. They seem truer than anything I have ever read. And they certainly turn the world upside down.

KATHERINE BUTLER HATHAWAY

It is more blessed to give than to receive.

ACTS 20:35 NIV

~~~

If we raise our children to be givers, everything they do will be blessed because God keeps His promises.

BONNIE JENSEN

~~~

We live in the present, we dream of the future, but we learn eternal truths from the past.

LUCY MAUD MONTGOMERY

~~~

God…never changes or casts a shifting shadow. He chose to give birth to us by giving us his true word. And we, out of all creation, became his prized possession.

JAMES 1:17-18 NLT

It is an extraordinary and beautiful thing that God, in creation…works with the beauty of matter; the reality of things; the discoveries of the senses, all five of them; so that we, in turn, may hear the grass growing; see a face springing to life in love and laughter.… The offerings of creation…our glimpses of truth.

Madeleine L'Engle

We don't want to limit what God can do in our children by trying to parent them alone. Trust God to take care of them.

Stormie Omartian

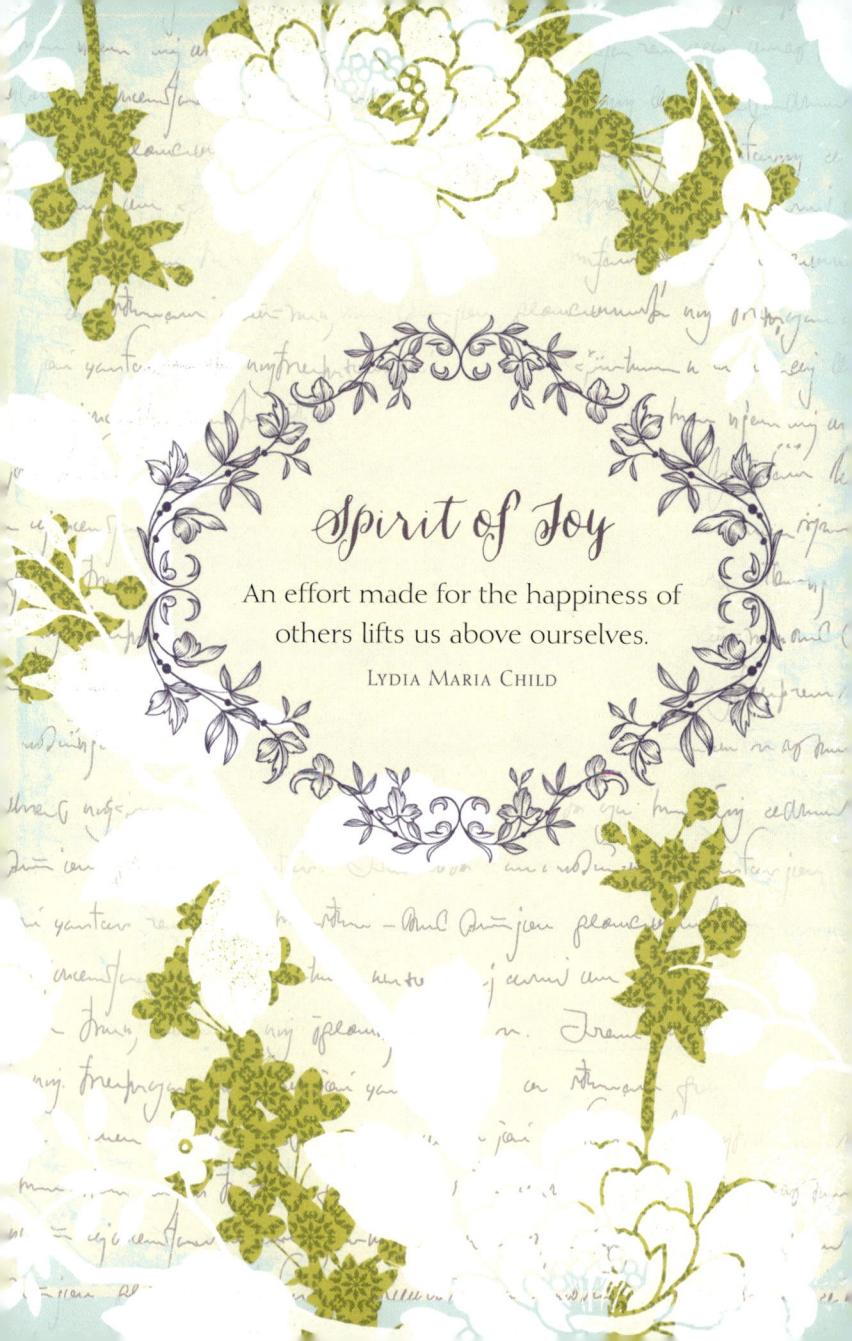

Spirit of Joy

An effort made for the happiness of
others lifts us above ourselves.

Lydia Maria Child

*H*ow necessary it is to cultivate a spirit of joy.
It is a psychological truth that the physical acts
of reverence and devotion make one feel devout.
The courteous gesture increases one's respect for
others. To act lovingly is to begin to feel loving,
and certainly to act joyfully brings joy to others
which in turn makes one feel joyful. I believe we
are called to the duty of delight.

DOROTHY DAY

---

*Sometimes the laughter in mothering
is the recognition of the ironies
and absurdities. Sometime, though,
it's just pure, unthinking delight.*

BARBARA SCHAPIRO

---

*M*y heart exults and triumphs in the Lord;
my horn (my strength) is lifted up in the Lord.
My mouth is no longer silent.

1 SAMUEL 2:1 AMP

Our hearts were made for joy. Our hearts were made to enjoy the One who created them. Too deeply planted to be much affected by the ups and downs of life, this joy is a knowing and a being known by our Creator. He sets our hearts alight with radiant joy.

Joy is warm and radiant and clamors for expressions and experience.

DOROTHY SEGOVIA

If one is joyful, it means that one is faithfully living for God, and that nothing else counts; and if one gives joy to others one is doing God's work. With joy without and joy within, all is well.

JANET ERSKINE STUART

*If a child is to keep his inborn sense of wonder…
he needs the companionship of at least one adult
who can share it, rediscovering with him the joy,
excitement, and mystery of the world we live in.*

RACHEL CARSON

---

*To be able to find joy in another's joy,
that is the secret of happiness.*

---

*Loving Creator, help me reawaken my childlike
sense of wonder at the delights of Your world!*

MARILYN MORGAN HELLEBERG

---

*All who seek the LORD will praise Him.
Their hearts will rejoice with everlasting joy.*

PSALM 22:26 NLT

My hope for you today: a double helping
of laughter, a cup full of love,
a heart brimming with joy!

❦

When hands reach out in friendship,
hearts are touched with joy.

❦

*Joy is the feeling of
grinning on the inside.*

MELBA COLGROVE

❦

God knows everything about us. And He cares
about everything. Moreover, He can manage
every situation. And He loves us! Surely this
is enough to open the wellsprings of joy....
Joy is always a source of strength.

HANNAH WHITALL SMITH

As we grow in our capacities to see and enjoy
the joys that God has placed in our lives,
life becomes a glorious experience
of discovering His endless wonders.

―※―

The Lord is my strength and my shield;
my heart trusts in him, and he helps me. My heart
leaps for joy, and with my song I praise him.

Psalm 28:7 niv

―※―

Since you get more joy out of giving joy
to others, you should put a good deal of thought
into the happiness that you are able to give.

Eleanor Roosevelt

To Live, Laugh, and Love

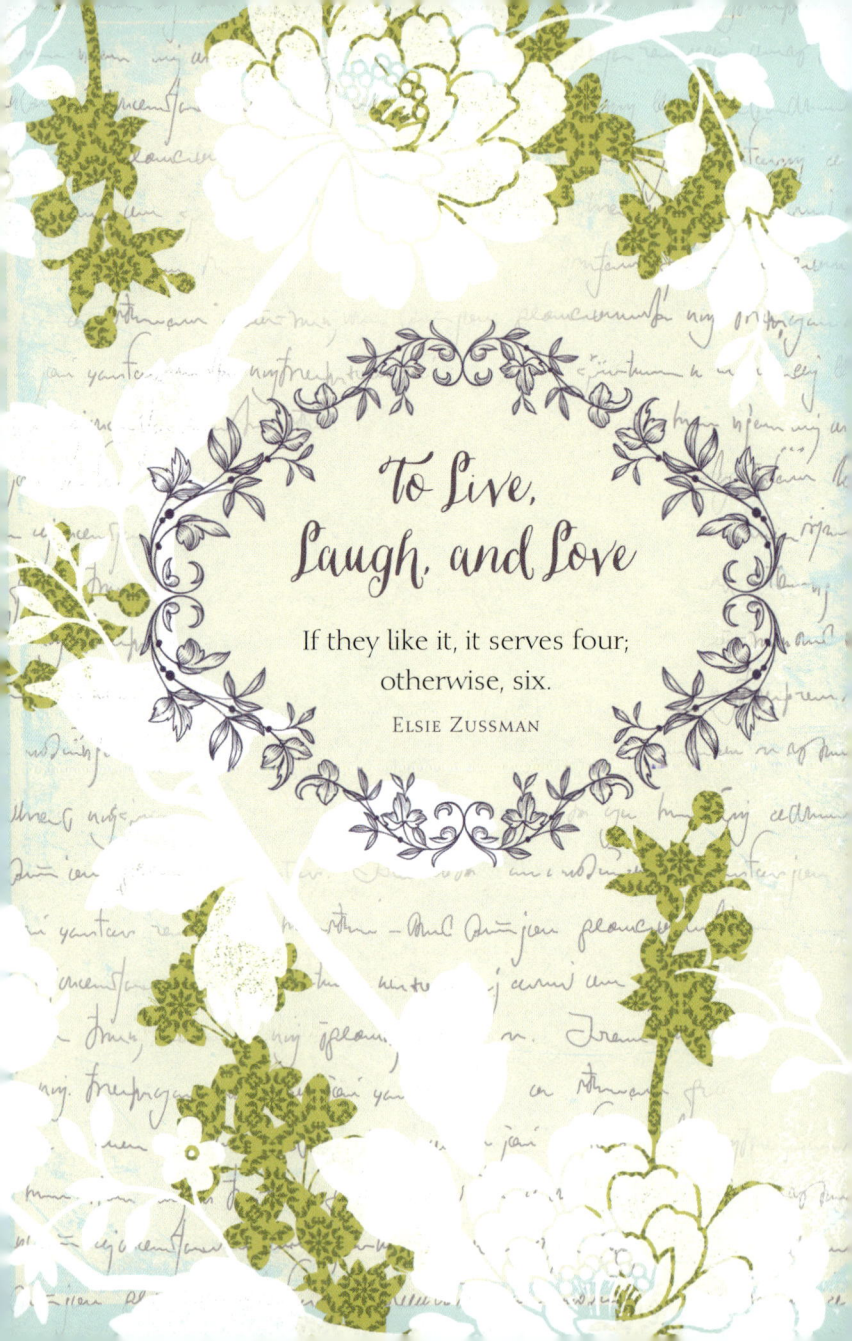

If they like it, it serves four;
otherwise, six.

ELSIE ZUSSMAN

Whole-hearted, ready laughter heals,
encourages, relaxes anyone within hearing
distance. The laughter that springs from
love makes wide the space around—gives room
for the loved one to enter in.

EUGENIA PRICE

A cheerful look brings joy to the heart;
good news makes for good health.

PROVERBS 15:30 NLT

*If it weren't for the last minute,
nothing would get done.*

One of the great joys of motherhood
is the happiness our children bring into our lives.
Let's make the effort to experience the laughter
of childhood with our children.

KIM BOYCE

Children seldom misquote you.
They more often repeat word for word
what you shouldn't have said.

MAE MALOO

Laugh at yourself first before anyone else can.

ELSA MAXWELL

People can be divided into three groups:
Those who make things happen,
those who watch things happen,
and those who wonder what happened.

Sense of humor; God's great gift
causes spirits to uplift,
Helps to make our bodies mend;
lightens burdens; cheers a friend;
Tickles children; elders grin
at this warmth that glows within;
Surely in the great hereafter
heaven must be full of laughter!

The mother of boys works son-up to son-down.

*If you can learn to laugh in spite
of the circumstances that surround you,
you will enrich others, enrich yourself,
and more than that, you will last!*

BARBARA JOHNSON

---

*When children's eyes are smiling
'Tis God's love that's shining through
With glints of joy and laughter
What good medicine for you!*

MARGARET FISHBACK POWERS

---

*May all who search for you be filled
with joy and gladness in you.*

PSALM 40:16 NLT

---

*Now, as always, the most automated
appliance in the household is the mother.*

BEVERLY JONES

The Strength of Family

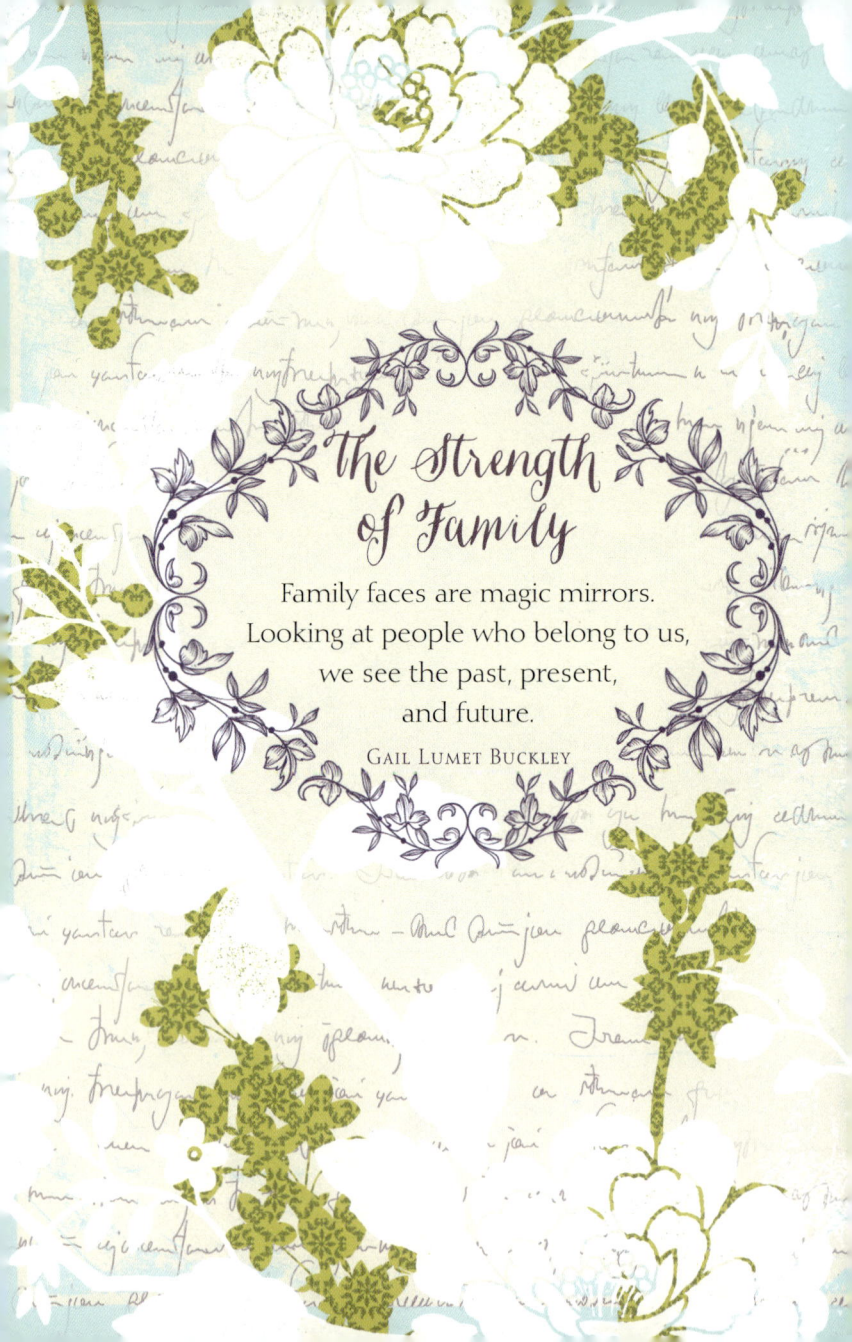

Family faces are magic mirrors.
Looking at people who belong to us,
we see the past, present,
and future.

GAIL LUMET BUCKLEY

A Mother's love is something that
no one can explain, it is made of deep
devotion and of sacrifice and pain.... It believes
beyond believing when the world around
condemns, and it glows with all the beauty
of the rarest, brightest gems.

Helen Steiner Rice

Mother is a verb, not a noun.

Who am I, O Lord God, and what is my family,
that you have brought me this far? And now,
O God, in addition to everything else,
you speak of giving your servant a lasting dynasty!
You speak as though I were someone very great,
O Lord God!

1 Chronicles 17:16–17 nlt

We were a strange little band of characters, trudging through life sharing diseases and toothpaste, coveting one another's desserts, hiding shampoo, borrowing money, locking each other out of our rooms, inflicting pain and kissing to heal it in the same instant, loving, laughing, defending, and trying to figure out the common thread that bound us all together.

Erma Bombeck

Call it clan, call it a network, call it a tribe, call it a family. Whatever you call it, whoever you are, you need one.

Jane Howard

Families give us many things—
love and meaning, purpose and an opportunity to give, and a sense of humor.

I hope my children look back on today and see a mom who had time to play. There will be years for cleaning and cooking, for children grow up while we're not looking.

We really need only five things on this earth: some food, some sun, some work, some fun, and someone.
— Beatrice Nolan

*A*sk any four-year-old boy, "Who's the most beautiful woman in the world?" His mommy! Ask any grown daughter caring for her aging mother the same question, and you'll get the same answer.

Sooner or later we all discover that
the important moments in life are not
the advertised ones, not the birthdays,
the graduations, the weddings,
not the great goals achieved.
The real milestones are less prepossessing.
They come to the door of memory.

SUSAN B. ANTHONY

The effect of having other interests beyond
those domestic works well. The more one does
and sees and feels, the more one is able to do,
and the more genuine may be one's appreciation
of fundamental things like home, and love,
and understanding companionship.

AMELIA EARHART

As for me and my house, we will serve the LORD.

JOSHUA 24:15 NKJV

If there be one thing pure...that can endure,
when all else passes away...it is a mother's love.

MARCHIONESS DE SPADARA

*Finally, all of you, be like-minded,
be sympathetic, love one another,
be compassionate and humble.*

1 PETER 3:8 NIV

Women know the way to rear up children
(to be just); they know a simple, merry,
tender knack of tying sashes, fitting baby-shoes,
and stringing pretty words that make no sense,
and kissing full sense into empty words;
which things are corals to cut life upon,
although such trifles.

ELIZABETH BARRETT BROWNING

I Believe

Faith allows us to continually delight
in life since we have placed
our needs in God's hands.

*I believe in the sun even if it isn't shining.
I believe in love even when I am alone.
I believe in God even when He is silent.*

Faith sees the invisible, believes the incredible, and receives the impossible.

Your mercy, O Lord, is in the heavens;
Your faithfulness reaches to the clouds.

PSALM 36:5 NKJV

Within each of us there is an inner place where the living God Himself longs to dwell, our sacred center of belief.

Faith is not an effort, a striving, a ceaseless seeking, as so many earnest souls suppose, but rather a letting go, an abandonment, an abiding rest in God that nothing, not even the soul's shortcomings, can disturb.

❦

I think miracles exist in part as gifts and in part as clues that there is something beyond the flat world we see.

PEGGY NOONAN

❦

Watch, stand fast in the faith, be brave, be strong.

1 CORINTHIANS 16:13 NKJV

If it can be verified, we don't need faith.... Faith is for that which lies on the other side of reason. Faith is what makes life bearable, with all its tragedies and ambiguities and sudden, startling joys.

MADELEINE L'ENGLE

Christ will make his home in your hearts as you trust in him. Your roots will grow down into God's love and keep you strong.

EPHESIANS 3:17 NLT

Not everyone possesses boundless energy or a conspicuous talent. We are not equally blessed with great intellect or physical beauty or emotional strength. But we have all been given the same ability to be faithful.

GIGI GRAHAM TCHIVIDJIAN

I see Heaven's glories shine, and faith shines equal, arming me from fear.

EMILY BRONTË

True faith drops its letter in the post office box and lets it go. Distrust holds on to a corner of it and wonders that the answer never comes.

L. B. COWMAN

Faith expects from God what is beyond all expectations.

If children feel love and acceptance from us, their view of God's love is strengthened. The world will give them opportunities to doubt— we must give them every reason to believe.

BONNIE JENSEN

Finding acceptance with joy, whatever the circumstances of life—whether they are petty annoyances or fiery trials—this is a living faith that grows.

MARY LOU STEIGLEDER

Faith means being sure of what we hope for... now. It means knowing something is real, this moment, all around you, even when you don't see it. Great faith isn't the ability to believe long and far into the misty future. It's simply taking God at His word and taking the next step.

JONI EARECKSON TADA

Be Encouraged

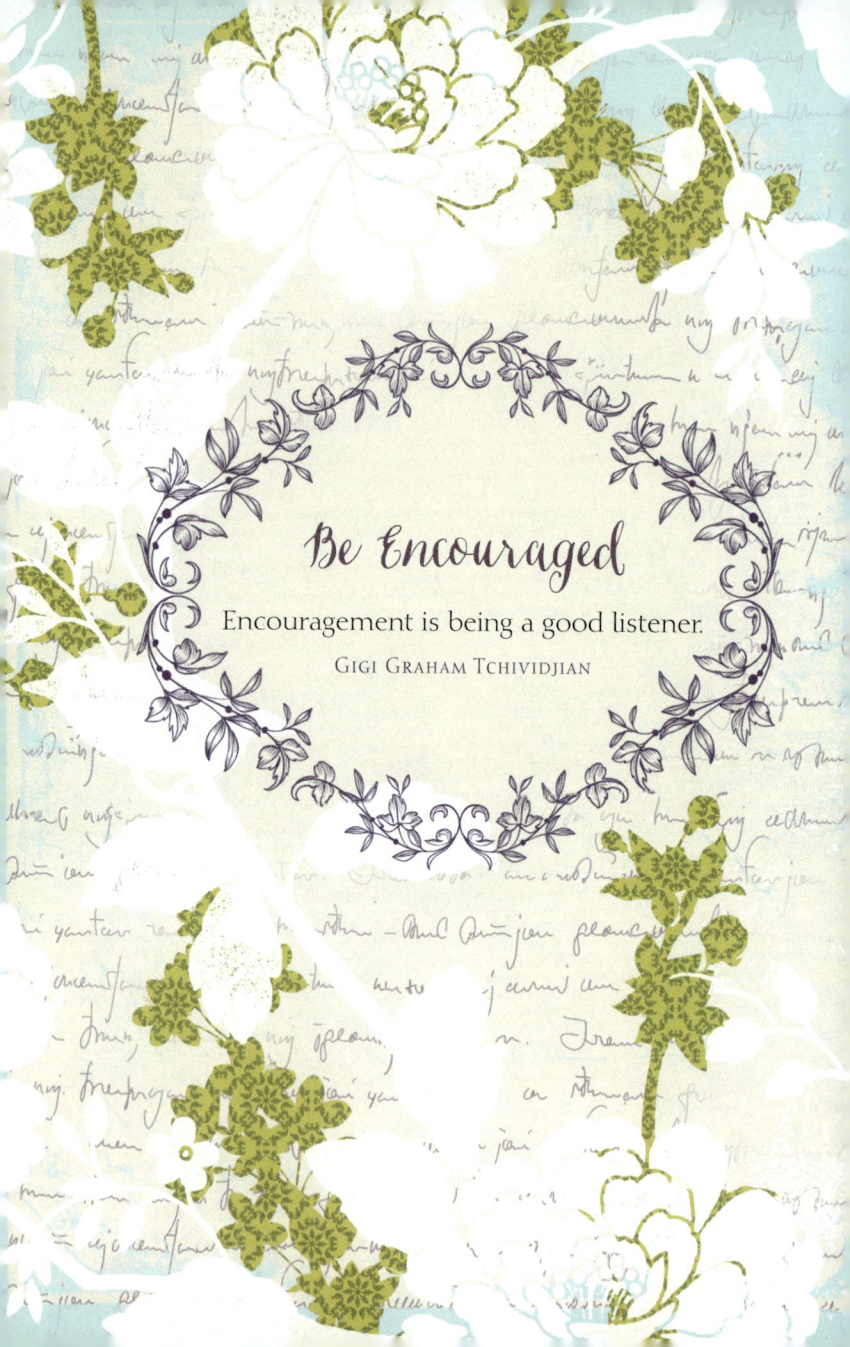

Encouragement is being a good listener.

GIGI GRAHAM TCHIVIDJIAN

There is not enough darkness in all the world
to put out the light of one small candle....
In moments of discouragement, defeat,
or even despair, there are always certain
things to cling to. Little things usually:
remembered laughter, the face of a sleeping child,
a tree in the wind—in fact, any reminder
of something deeply felt or dearly loved.

Arthur Gordon

*For we have great joy and consolation
in your love, because the hearts
of the saints have been refreshed by you.*

Philemon 1:7 NKJV

Being taken for granted can be a compliment.
It means that you've become a comfortable,
trusted person in another person's life.

Joyce Brothers

A word of encouragement to those we meet,
a cheerful smile in the supermarket, a card
or letter to a friend, a readiness to witness when
opportunity is given—all are practical ways
in which we may let His light shine through us.

Elizabeth B. Jones

God, bless all young mothers at end of day.
Kneeling wearily with each small one to hear
them pray. Too tired to rise when done…and yet
they do; longing just to sleep one whole night
through. Too tired to sleep…. Too tired to pray….
God, bless all young mothers at close of day.

Ruth Bell Graham

I wanted you to see what real courage is….
It's when you know you're licked before you
begin but you begin anyway and you see it
through no matter what.

Harper Lee

A mother is someone who dreams great
dreams for you, but then she lets you chase
the dreams you have for yourself and loves you
just the same. In the end, she believes in your
dreams as much as you do.

*The stars exist that we might know
how high our dreams can soar.*

Hope begins in the dark, the stubborn hope
that if you just show up and try to do
the right thing, the dawn will come. You wait
and watch and work: you don't give up.

ANNE LAMOTT

I remain confident of this:
I will see the goodness of the Lord
in the land of the living.

PSALM 27:13 NIV

Calm me, O Lord, as You stilled the storm,
still me, O Lord, keep me from harm.
Let all the tumult within me cease,
enfold me, Lord, in Your peace.

CELTIC TRADITIONAL

*At night I turn my problems
over to God. He's going
to be up all night anyway.*

CARRIE WESTINGSON

The Scriptures give us hope and encouragement as we wait patiently for God's promises to be fulfilled. May God, who gives this patience and encouragement, help you live in complete harmony with each other.

ROMANS 15:4–5 NLT

There are times when encouragement means
such a lot. And a word is enough to convey it.

GRACE STRICKER DAWSON

A mother is one who knows you
as you really are, understands where
you've been, accepts who you've become,
and still gently invites you to grow.

Some days, it is enough encouragement
just to watch the clouds break up and disappear,
leaving behind a blue patch of sky and bright
sunshine that is so warm upon my face.
It's a glimpse of divinity; a kiss from heaven.

Special Gifts We Share

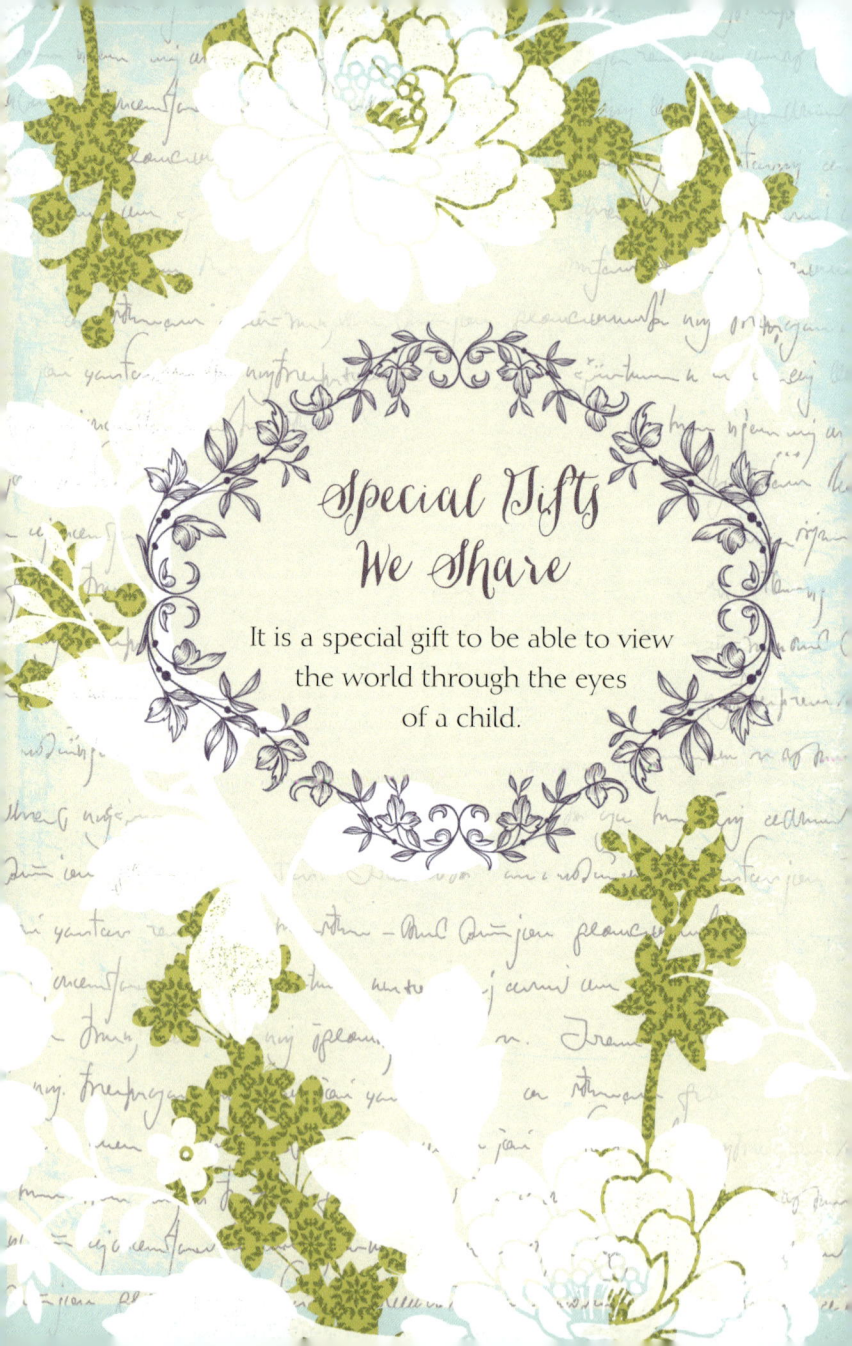

It is a special gift to be able to view the world through the eyes of a child.

Oh God, You have given me...a life of clay.
Put Your big hands around mine and guide
my hands so that every time I make a mark
on this life, it will be Your mark.

GLORIA GAITHER

*God does not ask your ability
or your inability. He asks
only your availability.*

MARY KAY ASH

It is good for people to eat, drink,
and enjoy their work under the sun during
the short life God has given them, and to accept
their lot in life. And it is a good thing to receive
wealth from God and the good health to enjoy it.
To enjoy your work and accept your lot in life—
this is indeed a gift from God.

ECCLESIASTES 5:18-19 NLT

Since you are like no other being ever created since the beginning of time, you are incomparable.

BRENDA UELAND

❧

Heavenly Father, thank You for the unique personalities that You have given to each and every child. Help me to discover each talent and gift with which You have blessed my children, and may I learn how to best cultivate each of the blossoms You have planted within their souls. Amen.

KIM BOYCE

❧

God gave me my gifts. I will do all I can to show Him how grateful I am to Him.

GRACE LIVINGSTON HILL

As Jesus looked up, he saw the rich putting their
gifts into the temple treasury. He also saw
a poor widow put in two very small copper coins.
"Truly I tell you," he said, "this poor widow
has put in more than all the others."

LUKE 21:1–3 NIV

Maybe all I could do was mother.... And yet,
why did I feel so fulfilled when I bedded down
three kids between clean sheets? What if raising
and instilling values in three children and turning
them into worthwhile human beings would
be the most important contribution
I ever made in my lifetime?

ERMA BOMBECK

Give, and it will be given to you. A good measure, pressed down, shaken together and running over, will be poured into your lap. For with the measure you use, it will be measured to you.

LUKE 6:38 NIV

~

Our greatest responsibility today may be the unselfish sacrifice of our time, talent, and love in the lives of those little ones around us.

SUSAN DOWNS

~

God's designs regarding you, and His methods of bringing about these designs, are infinitely wise.

MADAME JEANNE GUYON

~

This is the real gift: you have been given the breath of life, designed with a unique, one-of-a-kind soul that exists forever—the way that you choose to live it doesn't change the fact that you've been given the gift of being now and forever. Priceless in value, you are handcrafted by God.

Whatever job I perform—whether changing
a diaper, closing a deal, teaching a class,
or writing a book—when I meet legitimate needs,
I am carrying on God's work.

KATHY PEEL

Each one of us is God's special work
of art. Through us, He teaches
and inspires, delights and encourages,
informs and uplifts all those
who view our lives.

JONI EARECKSON TADA

I'll show my children right from wrong, encourage dreams and hope; explain respect for others, while teaching them to cope with outside pressures, inside fears, a world that's less than whole; and through it all I'll nurture my children's most precious soul! Though oftentimes a struggle, this job I'll never trade; for in my hand tomorrow lives…a future God has made.

Love Eternal

No one ever outgrows the need
for a mother's love.

My mother and I have laughed over nothing
and cried over everything. We understand each
other's fears, losses, and sense of humor.
She holds my heart like no one else can.

JANETTE OKE

The human heart, at whatever age,
opens only to the heart that opens in return.

MARIA EDGEWORTH

*Only He who created the wonders
of the world entwines hearts
in an eternal way.*

The Lord is good and his love endures forever;
his faithfulness continues through all generation.

PSALM 100:5 NIV

There is no need to plead that the love of God shall fill our hearts as though He were unwilling to fill us.... Love is pressing around us on all sides like air. Cease to resist it and instantly love takes possession.

AMY CARMICHAEL

You gave me life and showed me your unfailing love. My life was preserved by your care.

JOB 10:12 NLT

You have to love your children unselfishly. That's hard. But it's the only way.

BARBARA BUSH

Love grows from our capacity to give what is deepest within ourselves and also receive what is the deepest within another person. The heart becomes an ocean strong and deep, launching all on its tide. Being a full-time mother is one of the highest-salaried jobs in any field since the payment is pure love.

Mildred B. Vermont

Nothing can separate you from His love, absolutely nothing.... God is enough for time, and God is enough for eternity. God is enough!

Hannah Whitall Smith

Love the Lord God with all your passion
and prayer and intelligence and energy.

MARK 12:30 MSG

To love by freely giving is its own reward.
To be possessed by love and to in turn give
love away is to find the secret of abundant life.

GLORIA GAITHER

A mother's love is the heart of the home.
Her children's sense of security and self-worth
are found there. God will never let you be shaken
or moved from your place near His heart.

JONI EARECKSON TADA

*O*pen your hearts to the love God instills....
God loves you tenderly. What He gives you is not
to be kept under lock and key, but to be shared.

MOTHER TERESA

---

*B*efore you were conceived I wanted you
Before you were born I loved you
Before you were here an hour I would die for you
This is the miracle of life.

MAUREEN HAWKINS

What we have once enjoyed we can never lose. All that we love deeply becomes a part of us.

HELEN KELLER

I love you.

Always and forever.

The end.